PATRIOTIC
Little Quilts

ALICE BERG ★ SYLVIA JOHNSON
MARY ELLEN VON HOLT

Martingale™
& COMPANY

CREDITS

President . . . . Nancy J. Martin
CEO . . . . Daniel J. Martin
Publisher . . . . Jane Hamada
Editorial Director . . . . Mary V. Green
Managing Editor . . . . Tina Cook
Technical Editor . . . . Laurie Baker
Copy Editor . . . . Ellen Balstad
Design Director . . . . Stan Green
Technical Illustrator . . . . Laurel Strand
Decorative-Art Illustrator . . . . Edie Harlin
Cover Designer . . . . Stan Green
Text Designer . . . . Regina Girard
Photographers . . . . Brent Kane
David Dawson
Jason Wolf

That Patchwork Place® is an imprint
of Martingale & Company™.

Patriotic Little Quilts
© 2002 by Alice Berg, Sylvia Johnson,
and Mary Ellen Von Holt

Martingale & Company
20205 144th Avenue NE
Woodinville, WA 98072-8478 USA
www.martingale-pub.com

Printed in Hong Kong
07 06 05 04 03 02   8 7 6 5 4 3 2 1

Library of Congress Cataloging-in-Publication Data
Berg, Alice
    Patriotic little quilts / Alice Berg, Sylvia Johnson,
Mary Ellen Von Holt.
        p. cm.
    ISBN 1-56477-456-2
1. Patchwork—Patterns. 2. Quilting—Patterns.
3. Appliqué—Patterns. 4. Patriotism in art. I. Johnson,
Sylvia. II. Von Holt, Mary Ellen. III. Title.
    TT835 .B3564 2002
    746.46'041—dc21
                                        2002007830

MISSION STATEMENT

We are dedicated to providing quality products and service by working
together to inspire creativity and to enrich the lives we touch.

Dedication

To the families of those lost on September 11, 2001,
and the quilters who responded to our request so generously.

Acknowledgments

We wish to thank:

⭐ Anne Anderberg ⭐ Libby Lowe ⭐ Wanda Hizer ⭐ Jennie Suter ⭐

⭐ Tina Schuman ⭐ Mildred Moss ⭐ Laura Edwards ⭐

⭐ Maria Peagler ⭐ Deborah Mix ⭐ Lone Gade Christensen ⭐

⭐ Julie Pierce, Atlanta Sewing Center of Atlanta, Georgia ⭐

⭐ The staff at Little Quilts ⭐

⭐ Dave Dawson Photography of Atlanta, Georgia ⭐

⭐ Jason Wolf Photography of Marietta, Georgia ⭐

⭐ Edie Harlin, illustrator ⭐

⭐ The quilters featured in the gallery ⭐

⭐ Marietta, Georgia, Fire Station #2 ⭐

Contents

A Note from the Authors

At Little Quilts®, we have been blessed over the years with the chance to make friends with quilters, not only in our country but across the world. Through our books and publications we have brought our idea of decorating homes with small quilts to places we never dreamed possible. What began as a wholesale business for our patterns, kits, and booklets has grown to include a fabric line with Peter Pan Fabrics and a retail store, Little Quilts, which we opened on November 3, 1998, in Marietta, Georgia.

Showing our love of country and being patriotic has always been a natural part of our lives. Red, white, and denim are our basic wardrobe colors! We enjoy purchasing folk art with an Americana theme and decorating our homes with antique memorabilia, such as well-worn flags and vintage needlework. Flags wave outside our homes and store. There is always a Fourth of July party to attend, and in years past, Sylvia has participated in the Peachtree Road Race on that morning. Our store always features fabrics, patterns, and books with patriotic designs. Being spirited about our country is happy and exciting for us and we hope that the spirit in this book will bring you much delight.

⭐ *Alice Berg, Mary Ellen Von Holt, and Sylvia Johnson* ⭐

Introduction

The terrorist attacks against the United States on September 11, 2001, had a profound effect on everyone, no matter what country she or he lived in. People wanted to do something, but aside from making donations, they felt helpless due to the scope of the situation.

On September 13, 2001, we at Little Quilts sent an e-mail to approximately one thousand of our e-mail newsletter subscribers, asking each of them to make a little red-white-and-blue quilt and send it to us. We explained our plan to send all of the quilts we received to New York and give them to the families of the firefighters, police officers, and emergency workers who were lost in the tragedy. We asked everyone who wanted to participate to make their quilt fast, make it simple, and make it sweet. We set the deadline for October 11, 2001.

The response to our e-mail request was overwhelming, both emotionally and in the number of quilts we were entrusted with. We expected to receive several hundred quilts. More than twenty-three hundred quilts arrived, some with letters of thanks for giving quilters this opportunity to express their feelings. The quilts were made by beginning and professional quilters, Boy Scouts, Girl Scouts, children, office workers, and many more. The quilts came from almost every state, as well as several foreign countries. As we looked at the quilts, we realized how special they were and what each one represented.

Writing this book gives us the opportunity to do two things. First, we are able to pay tribute to the quilters from around the world who answered our e-mail. We regret that we can't show all of the quilts that were sent to us, but you can see some of them in "Gallery of American Tribute Quilts" on pages 20–25. With the help of many, we distributed the quilts and moved on, knowing that we had extended the hand of friendship through these small quilts. Second, we are able to share the inspiration of these quilts and this experience by providing patriotic quilt projects for you to make for your home, office, or as gifts. You'll find directions for fifteen patriotic Little Quilts starting on page 26, with basic instructions, helpful tips, and some of our favorite shortcuts to create them starting on page 9.

Our parking lot and hearts were filled with warmth at the outpouring of quilts received from our request.

What Is a Little Quilt?

In our previous books, *Little Quilts All through the House* and *Celebrate! with Little Quilts*, published by Martingale & Company, we have shared our idea of making small, not miniature, quilts based on traditional designs. These quilts are made just like a large quilt, consisting of quilt blocks, borders, quilting, and binding. The piece sizes are easy to handle and you can incorporate any new techniques that are appropriate to help with construction.

You will need only simple, basic supplies and small amounts of a variety of fabrics. These small quilts can be used in many decorative ways throughout your home. Make one for yourself and one to give. They really are a lot of fun!

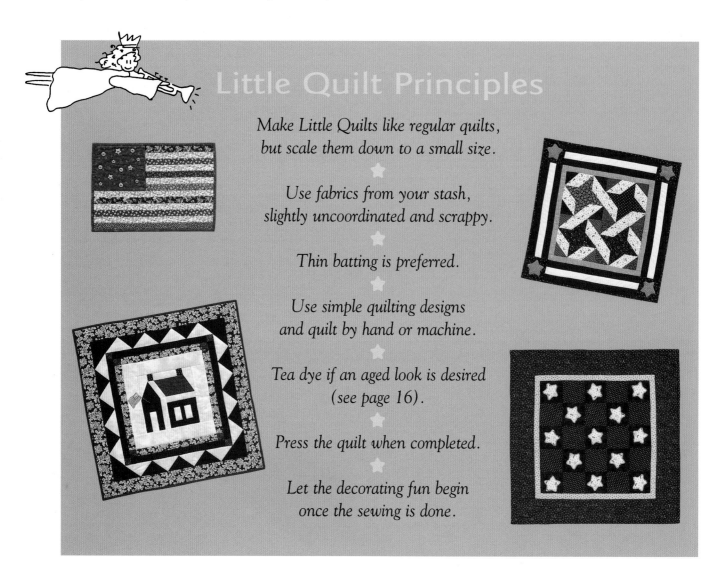

Little Quilt Principles

Make Little Quilts like regular quilts, but scale them down to a small size.

Use fabrics from your stash, slightly uncoordinated and scrappy.

Thin batting is preferred.

Use simple quilting designs and quilt by hand or machine.

Tea dye if an aged look is desired (see page 16).

Press the quilt when completed.

Let the decorating fun begin once the sewing is done.

Let's Get Started!

CHOOSING FABRICS

Choosing fabrics often can be a dilemma, but when making patriotic quilts it's easy to begin fabric selection by thinking about the bright, clear colors represented in the flag. Use those same hues or think a bit further about each color. Red, for example, can be burgundy, raspberry, or a darker shade of pink. The same idea applies to the color blue. White is effectively replaced by tan or shirting prints that have a neutral background and a small print.

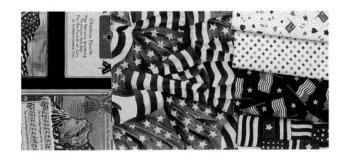

There are also a great number of fabrics with patriotic themes printed on them. Fabrics printed with flags, stars, stripes, fireworks, and more offer endless opportunities to add to the excitement of the quilt. Pay careful attention when using conversational prints, however. Partner them with other prints, such as plaids, checks, and small geometrics that read as solid so that the block design does not become lost in the process.

See how the fabrics in the block on the left stand alone to create a simple four-patch design, while the fabrics in the block on the right blur together and lose the design.

A patriotic theme taken from a song, pledge, or elsewhere also can inspire the colors used in a quilt. Words from the song "America the Beautiful" were the inspiration for our quilt "Purple Mountain Majesties" (page 56). Let your imagination run free as you express yourself in the quilt.

Most of the quilt projects in this book are scrap quilts that use many different fabrics in small amounts. The use of assorted fabrics in similar shades is the secret to a beautiful scrap quilt, large or small. If you don't already have a stash of scraps, build your collection by purchasing fat quarters (18" x 22" pieces) or half-yard pieces. Many quilt shops put together bundles of small amounts of coordinating fabrics to aid quilters in the decision-making process.

Stretch your patriotic palette by purchasing small amounts of different fabrics.

One fun idea to use when making a scrap quilt is to pretend that you ran out of a particular fabric and must substitute it with a close replacement. Many quilters who enjoy reproducing antique quilts make blocks with subtle substitutions.

SELECTING BATTING

We use thin cotton batting for most Little Quilts. This product has been improved so much that it has become a staple for us for both hand and machine quilting. Other types of batting, such as polyester or wool, are fine to use, but make sure they're not too fluffy! A high-loft batting does not achieve the Little Quilts look. Follow the manufacturer's directions for preparation and care.

GATHERING SUPPLIES AND EQUIPMENT

The supplies needed to make Little Quilts are no different than those needed for larger quilts. Following are some suggestions for items we use frequently and that make the quilting process easier. If you need help selecting tools or equipment, be sure to visit your local quilt shop for advice.

⭐ Neutral color thread, such as tan or gray, for piecing; matching color thread for appliqué

⭐ A sewing machine in good working order. If you haven't taken it in for a "physical" lately, maybe now is the time.

⭐ Rotary cutter, cutting mat, and rulers for cutting strips and other pieces

⭐ Fine-line, water-soluble marker to transfer embroidery designs to the fabric

⭐ Buttons for embellishing

⭐ Basic sewing supplies, including scissors, pins, needles, embroidery floss, and an iron

MAKING A DESIGN WALL

A design wall made of cotton flannel or polyester fleece is invaluable when constructing a quilt of any size, especially a Little Quilt. You can arrange blocks on the wall and then stand back to see how they look. It's easy to audition borders for your project on the wall too.

To make a design wall, purchase 1½ yards of flannel or fleece. Tack or tape the fleece to a wall. If you do not have a spare wall, cover a large piece of plywood or foam-core board (available from an art-supply store). You can easily store this board when it is not in use.

General Directions

These Little Quilts are easy to make, and we want you to enjoy yourself. Projects give rotary-cutting and machine-piecing instructions. Template patterns are provided, starting on page 89, if you wish to hand piece or check your rotary-cut pieces. All measurements include ¼"-wide seam allowances, unless otherwise specified.

ROTARY CUTTING

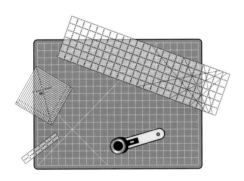

You can use a rotary cutter, acrylic ruler, and mat to accurately cut several layers of fabric at one time. These tools are invaluable when making multifabric quilts. Make sure your blade is sharp and that you keep your mat free of pins and other objects that could damage the blade. Keep the blade closed when the cutter is not in use.

For rotary-cutting techniques, consult *Shortcuts: A Concise Guide to Rotary Cutting* by Donna Lynn Thomas (Martingale & Company, 1999).

MACHINE PIECING

Learn to sew an accurate ¼" seam. Any variation in your ¼"-wide seam allowance will affect the size of your block. This in turn will affect the size of other quilt elements, such as sashing and borders.

Some machines have a special quilting foot that measures exactly ¼" from the center needle position to the edge of the foot. If your machine doesn't have this type of foot available, place the ¼" mark of an acrylic ruler under the needle, and then create a seam guide by placing the edge of a piece of tape, moleskin, or a magnetic seam guide along the edge of the ruler.

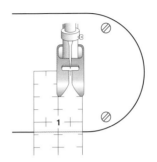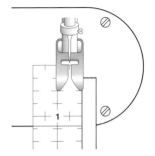

Use ¼" mark on acrylic ruler to locate a new seam guide.

Put masking tape in front of needle along edge of ruler to guide fabric.

Don't watch the needle go up and down as you sew. To our knowledge, one has never jumped off the machine and run away! Keep your eye on the fabric edges and how they are being fed into the machine. Use pins if needed to keep the fabrics together, but remove them as the needle approaches them. Keeping the edges of the fabric together, combined with good guiding, will make you a patchwork winner.

HAND PIECING

Hand piecing is like sewing together a patchwork puzzle, and accuracy is important for success. For hand piecing, trace the template patterns that start on page 89 onto template plastic, following the dashed lines marked on the inside of the patterns, not the outer solid line. Mark the grain line. Place each template on the wrong side of the appropriate fabric, paying attention to the fabric grain line, and trace around it with a sharp pencil. This drawn line is the actual sewing line. When cutting each piece, cut ¼" beyond this line to add the seam allowance.

Lay out the pieces, right side up, so you can see the design. You will sew small units together to make larger ones. Pin pieces together, matching seam lines. Sew on the lines, using a small running stitch; check to make sure you are stitching on the lines of both pieces. Only sew on the lines; seam

allowances must remain free. Trim seams to ⅛"
after sewing each one.

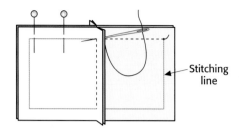

Stitching
line

PRESSING

It is important to press seams as you sew them.
Pressing makes it easier to match seams and helps
ensure that the finished block will be the correct
size.

After stitching the pieces together, press the
seams flat on the fabric wrong side first. This will
relax the stitching and keep the edges of the piece
from distorting. Then, working on the fabric right
side, press the seams in one direction, usually
toward the darker fabric.

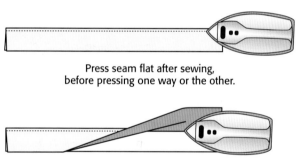

Press seam flat after sewing,
before pressing one way or the other.

Press seam in one direction.

APPLIQUÉING

Several of the projects in this book incorporate
appliquéd designs into the quilt top. You may
choose to hand appliqué the motifs or use fusible
appliqué methods. Appliqué patterns do not
include seam allowances. Templates can be made
using the appliqué patterns and template plastic or
freezer paper.

Hand Appliqué

Place the appliqué template right side up on the
right side of the fabric and trace around it. Cut ⅛"
to ¼" from this line. Turn under the seam
allowance and finger-press. Baste close to the edge
to hold the seam allowance in place.

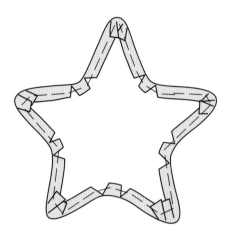

Clip only where necessary. Pin the pieces in
place, noting where one piece may overlap another. A seam allowance that is overlapped by another piece need not be basted under. A dotted line on
the appliqué pattern indicates overlapped areas.

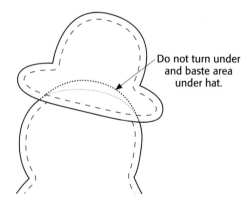

Do not turn under
and baste area
under hat.

Appliqué with a single thread in a color that
matches the appliqué piece. Sew the piece in place
with an appliqué stitch.

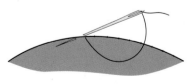

Appliqué Stitch

The needle-turn stitching method works well for simple shapes, such as leaves. Baste the shape to the background fabric about ⅛" inside the drawn line. Use the needle to turn under the seam allowance as you sew around the appliqué. Trim away the excess seam allowance as you sew.

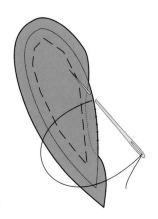

Fusible Appliqué

Many fusing products are available for applying one piece of fabric to another. You can use this method of quick appliqué to save time. Fabrics do stiffen after application, so choose a lightweight fusible web that you can stitch through. Follow the manufacturer's directions for the product you select. *You must reverse the appliqué templates when you trace around them on the paper side of the fusible web.*

EMBROIDERING

Several of the projects in this book feature small amounts of embroidery. You will work all stitches with two strands of embroidery floss and a sharp embroidery needle. Add stitched elements before adding borders.

Buttonhole Stitch

The buttonhole stitch can be both decorative and functional. If you fused your appliqué shapes in place, this stitch will not only add decorative appeal to the

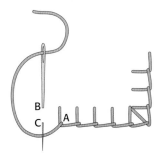

shapes, but it will also serve to hold them securely in place. Working from right to left, bring the needle up from the back to the front at A. Insert the needle back through the fabric at B. Slide it through to C, with the point of the needle over the thread. The line that connects the stitches should lie against the cut edge of the appliqué piece.

Cross-Stitch

Bring the needle up at A and down at B. Repeat to work all of the single slanting stitches in one row. Then come up at C and down at D, crossing the stitches, to complete each cross-stitch.

Double Cross-Stitch

The double cross-stitch is simply a regular cross-stitch with a straight cross-stitch imposed over it. Come up at A, down at B, up at C, down at D, up at E, down at F, up at G, and down at H.

French Knot

Bring the needle up at A, wrap the thread around the needle twice to form the knot, and reinsert at A.

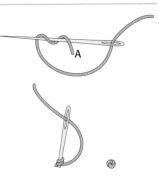

Stem Stitch

The stem stitch is one of the most frequently used embroidery

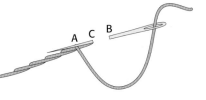

stitches. It is quite easy to work and is often used for outlining. To make the stem stitch, bring the needle up from the back to the front at A. Reinsert the needle at B and bring it out again at C as shown. Keep the embroidery floss under the needle as you take each stitch. The stitches should be even and equal in size.

Quilt Finishing

After you have assembled the Little Quilt top, it's time to add borders, layer with batting and backing, quilt, and then bind.

ADDING BORDERS

For best results, do not cut border strips and sew them directly to the quilt sides without measuring first. The edges of a quilt often measure slightly longer than the distance through the quilt center, due to stretching during construction. Instead, measure the quilt top through the center in both directions to determine how long to cut the border strips. This step ensures that the finished quilt will be as straight and as square as possible, without wavy edges. Refer to the following instructions to cut the strips to the required lengths and stitch them to the quilt top.

1. Measure the length of the quilt top through the vertical center. Cut 2 border strips to that measurement, piecing as necessary. Mark the center of the border strips and the quilt-top side edges.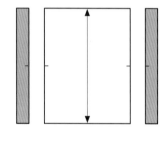

2. With right sides together, pin the borders to the sides of the quilt top, matching the center marks and ends. Stitch the borders in place, easing in any excess fabric as needed. Press the seams toward the border strips.

3. Measure the width of the quilt top through the horizontal center, including the side borders just added. Cut 2 border strips to that measurement, piecing as necessary. Mark the center of the border strips and the top and bottom edges of the quilt top.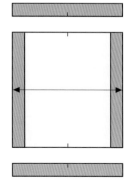

4. With right sides together, pin the borders to the top and bottom edges of the quilt top, matching center marks and ends. Stitch the borders in place, easing in any excess fabric as needed. Press the seams toward the border strips.

5. Add any additional borders in the same manner.

QUILTING

Quilting will slightly reduce the size of your finished quilt top. Mark quilting lines with an ordinary pencil, washable fabric marker, or white pencil. Cut backing fabric and batting a few inches larger than the quilt top all the way around. Layer the backing, batting, and quilt top; then baste the layers together. Thread basting works best for hand quilting. For machine quilting, use safety pins or a spray-basting product to temporarily hold the layers together.

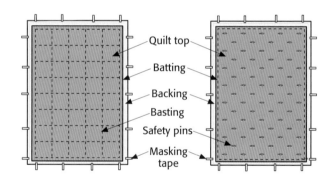

To quilt by hand, follow these steps:

1. Tie a single knot in the end of an 18" length of quilting thread.

2. Insert the needle in the top layer of the quilt about ½" from where you want to start quilting. Quilt from the center out to the edges and use a quilting hoop to hold the work whenever possible. Slide the needle through the batting and bring it out on the marked quilting line. Gently tug on the thread until the knot pops through the fabric, burying the knot in the batting.

3. Make small, even stitches through all layers, following your marked quilting lines.

Creative Borders

Patriotic quilts provide great possibilities for effective borders. The border can be very simple, made from a single fabric that coordinates with the quilt; pieced to look like stripes, flags, stars, and more; or decorated with appliqué, buttons, and embroidered embellishments. Here are some tips and suggestions for borders:

⭐ Use one fabric that "speaks" for the quilt—a conversation print, for example.

⭐ Cut borders along the lengthwise grain whenever possible for border strips with the least amount of stretch.

⭐ Not enough of the perfect fabric? Use random lengths of similar fabrics and connect them to make one strip long enough to go around the quilt.

⭐ Inner borders—usually thinner strips—are a resting place for the eyes. Use them as a way to accent a color in the quilt.

⭐ Use similar but different fabrics in your patchwork to add interest.

⭐ Make corner squares from patchwork blocks.

4. To end your stitches, make a single knot about ¼" from the quilt top. Take the next stitch but keep the needle between the fabric layers. Bring the needle out ½" from your last stitch and tug on the knot until it pops into the batting. Clip the thread and work it back into the quilt "sandwich."

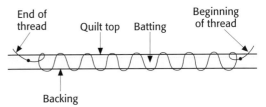

Many of the projects presented in this book are quilted "in the ditch," which means to quilt in the seam line of the block or patchwork shape. Quilt on the side opposite the seam allowances. This makes the quilting easier because there are fewer layers through which to stitch.

To quilt by machine, follow these steps:
1. Use a neutral-color nylon or matching-color thread made especially for machine quilting.
2. Attach a walking foot or even-feed foot to the machine so that the fabric layers feed evenly through the machine.

Refer to *Machine Quilting Made Easy* by Maurine Noble (Martingale & Company, 1994) for further assistance.

BINDING

This is an important step to finishing your quilt. Avoid using packaged bias binding. Make binding from fabrics used in the quilt or that coordinate well. You can make an interesting binding by joining random strips from fabrics used in the quilt.

To bind your quilt, follow these steps:
1. Trim the backing and batting even with the quilt-top edges.
2. Cut 1¼"-wide strips across the width of the binding fabric.
3. Join enough strips to go around the quilt, plus 4" to 6" extra.
4. Place binding on the quilt top with right sides together and raw edges even. Fold the beginning of the strip back ½" and pin.

5. Pin the binding to one side of the quilt at a time. Stitch through all the layers, using a ¼"-wide seam allowance. Stop stitching ¼" from the corner; backstitch. Clip threads and remove the piece from the machine. Fold the binding straight up and then straight down so that the binding edge is parallel to the next quilt edge. Stitch from the edge as shown.

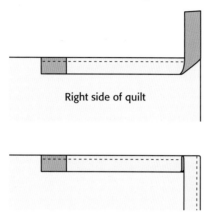

Right side of quilt

6. Repeat for each corner. When you reach the starting point, sew the end across the beginning fold. Cut off excess binding. Bring the raw edge over to the back, fold under ¼", and blindstitch in place, covering the machine stitching. Tuck corners to form a miter.

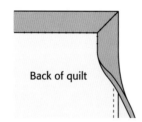

Back of quilt

TEA DYEING

Use a tea bath to give your quilt an aged look. This is our recipe for a simple tea bath.

Tea Dyeing Recipe

2 quarts *hot* tap water

6 to 8 tea bags

Place the tea bags in a large bowl. Pour the hot water over the bags and let steep for 15 minutes.

Remove the tea bags. Add the quilt and soak it in the tea solution for 15 to 30 minutes. Rinse the quilt in cool water. Squeeze out excess water. Lay the quilt flat to dry. Press the quilt to reshape.

EMBELLISHING WITH BUTTONS

Old and new buttons are fun to include on Little Quilts. There are even many star shapes available that would look charming on the patriotic projects in this book. Sew buttons on with embroidery floss after you complete the quilt.

LABELING

Your name, the quilt's name, the date the quilt was finished, and any other relevant information are an important part of your quilt. Creative labels are a lot of fun and a great way to record this information! Often leftover blocks can be used for this purpose. For your patriotic Little Quilt, we suggest making a small flag and writing the information on the stripes.

HANGING LITTLE QUILTS

⭐ Attach a fabric sleeve to the back and insert a lattice strip with holes in each end for hanging on small nails.

⭐ Attach two small, rustproof safety pins to the back of the quilt, close to the top; then hang on tiny nails.

⭐ Frame your Little Quilt.

Shortcuts

Many of the patchwork blocks used to make these patriotic Little Quilts are simple to construct with rotary-cutting and piecing shortcuts described in this section. It is always nice to know some tricks of the trade that will help you.

HALF-SQUARE TRIANGLES

Two right-angle triangles—also known as half-square triangles—are easy to rotary cut and machine piece into blocks. Determine the finished size of the short side of the triangle needed. Add $\frac{7}{8}$" to this measurement. Cut a square this size; then cut it once diagonally to yield two triangles. Sew pairs of triangles together along the long edges as shown, using an accurate $\frac{1}{4}$" seam allowance. Single half-square triangles are also used for corner triangles on diagonally set quilts. We often use printed foundation papers for making accurate half-square triangles. They are available in the notions section of quilt shops.

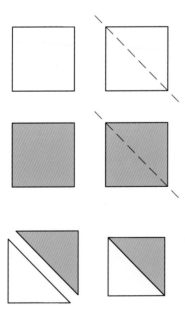

QUARTER-SQUARE TRIANGLES

Use quarter-square triangles for side setting triangles on diagonally set quilts. The straight of grain is on the outside or long edge of the triangle. To cut these triangles without a template, cut a square that is $1\frac{1}{4}$" larger than the finished long side of the triangle. Cut the square twice diagonally to yield four triangles.

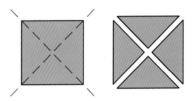

FOUR PATCH BLOCKS

To make Four Patch blocks, first choose same-width strips of fabric and sew them together in pairs. Use many short strips for variety. Press the seams toward the darker fabrics in each strip-pieced unit. Crosscut the sewn strips into segments the same width as a single strip of the strip set. For instance, if you joined two 2" strips together, cut the segments 2" wide. Join two segments to form each Four Patch block.

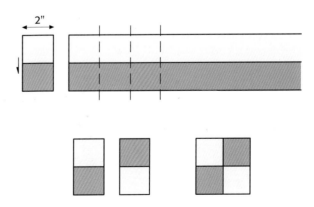

FLYING GEESE

Flying Geese blocks are easy to make using this shortcut method. For each unit, you will need one rectangle of fabric and two squares in a contrasting fabric in the sizes indicated in the project directions.

1. Draw a diagonal line from corner to corner on the wrong side of each square.

2. With right sides together, place a square on one end of the rectangle. Sew on the marked line. Trim the corner of the square, leaving a small seam allowance. Do not trim away the corner of the rectangle. Press the triangle toward the corner.

3. Place the second square on the opposite end of the rectangle, with the marked line as shown. Sew, trim, and press in the same manner as the first square.

SAWTOOTH STARS

Sawtooth Star blocks are simple to construct using four flying-geese units, one center square that is the same size as the longest side of the flying-geese units, and four corner squares that are the same size as the shortest side of the flying-geese units.

1. Refer to "Flying Geese" at left to construct 4 units.

2. Assemble the Sawtooth Star block as shown in the piecing diagram.

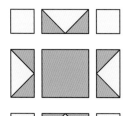 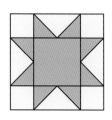

Make It Scrappy!

Creating a scrap quilt does not mean that you use any and every fabric. Planning before sewing is the secret to success. Making subtle substitutions with fabric can really create interest and give the viewer a lot to look at and study. Here is our way to make wonderful patchwork blocks with a scrappy look. We show the technique on a Sawtooth Star block, but you can see from the project photos that it works well with many blocks.

1. Gather an assortment of fabrics for the project. You will need dark- and medium-colored fabrics for the star and light-colored fabrics for the background. As you gain confidence, you can use a stronger background fabric. Always look for good contrast between the star and background fabrics.

2. Rotary cut the pieces for the block, using the measurements that follow to make a 6" block. A ¼" seam allowance is included in the measurements. You should cut at least 10 pieces from each fabric so you can get a feel for the substitution process. Save leftover pieces for future projects.

From the star fabrics, cut:
- 3½" x 3½" squares for center
- 2" x 2" squares for points

From the background fabrics, cut:
- 2" x 3½" rectangles
- 2" x 2" squares

3. Place the cut pieces—centers, points, and background—in groups in front of you, like a buffet.

4. Lay the pieces for each star on a sheet of white paper. Begin with 1 center square. Then arrange 8 background pieces around the square as shown. All of the background pieces should be from the same fabric. Choose 8 squares for the star points. Again, all of the pieces should be from the same fabric. You may not see a star at this stage, but you can get an idea of what the block will look like, and also check for contrast, if you fold a star-point square diagonally. Cut more pieces for the block "buffet" if needed.

5. Now the fun begins! Begin substituting a few pieces. Start with different background corners, and star points in the same color but with a different print. Make subtle changes, and don't change every piece.

6. Repeat this process on more sheets of paper until you have planned the blocks you will need for a quilt.

7. Place the papers on the floor and move them around to get an idea of how the quilt will look. Make any changes now.

8. Stack the papers and take them to your sewing machine. Refer to "Sawtooth Stars" on page 18 to sew the pieces together. Press well as you sew.

Gallery of American Tribute Quilts

The quilts featured in this gallery were made within a one-month period and sent to us for our New York project. We chose these quilts as representatives of the 2,300 quilts received. We are grateful to these quilters for participating in the project and this book.

Daryl Dowding, Tampa, Florida,
18" x 13½". Variation of "Celebration Flags" from
Little Quilts All through the House by Little Quilts.

Kathy Wagner, Ontario, Canada, 9½" x 9½".

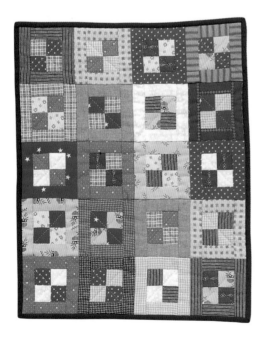

Virginia B. Kennedy, Jonesborough, Tennessee,
14" x 17½". Variation of "Framed Four Patch" from
Twenty Little Four-Patch Quilts by Gwen Marston.

JoAnne L. Reid, Scottsboro, Alabama, 24" x 24".
Variation of designs from *Combing through Your Scraps* by Karen Combs and *Around the Block* by Judy Hopkins.

Sandra Beyer, Baxter, Minnesota, 16" x 16".
Original design, with center embroidery
created by Amazing Designs.

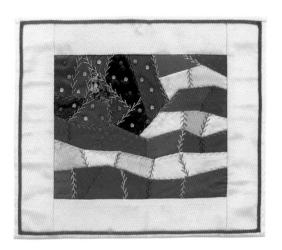

Lori Strablow, Palmyra, New York, 15½" x 12½".

Gail Hausler,
Summerville,
South Carolina,
8" x 8".

Nancy E. Nigh, Ontario, Canada, 19" x 24".
Based on a pattern by Diane Hansen from *Quilting
Ideas, Spring 2001* by Better Homes and Gardens.

Kayo Nakamura, Marietta, Georgia, 18" x 24".
Variation of "Sunbonnet Sue Sampler" from
Little Quilts All through the House by Little Quilts.

Holly Anderson,
Cumming, Georgia,
14" x 17½".

Lois D. Griffith, Cave Creek, Arizona, 23½" x 18".

Anne French, Toledo, Ohio, 20½" x 19".

Linda Bowser, Montgomery, Texas, 21" x 21".

Susan M. Hardin, Villa Rica, Georgia, 16½" x 21".
Adaptation of "Freedom Flight 1, 2, 3"
by Pine Tree Lodge Designs.

Kay Morrison, Centennial, Colorado, 17" x 23".

Randi Åse Mulelid, Asker, Norway, 10¾" x 14". "Cinnamon Hearts" from *Little Quilts All through the House* by Little Quilts.

Geraldine A. McBride, Rosemount, Minnesota, 14" x 14".

Selina Kapik, Kennesaw, Georgia, 21" x 16". Adaptation of a quilt in *Whimsies & Whynots* by Mary Lou Weidman.

Sylvia Strange, Chester, South Carolina, 12½" x 12½". Variation of "Lone Star Runner" from *Stars, Stripes, and Stitches* by Kasi Skelly and Jodi Barrows.

Dawn M. Benett, Suwanee, Georgia, 20" x 25".

Carol Krueger and Claudia M. Kieffer,
Hayward, Wisconsin, 19½" x 19½".

Mary Ann Ware, Bogart, Georgia, 17" x 13".
Variation of a free Web-site pattern
designed by Christine Treash © 2001.

Marvine Cole, Alpharetta, Georgia, 27" x 27".

Kathy L. Niemann, Marietta, Georgia, 24½" x 13".
Original design, with letters from *Two-Hour
Quilted Christmas Projects* by Cheri Saffiote.

Carol Matthews, Marietta, Georgia, 13½" x 15½".

Marcie Patch, Virginia Beach, Virginia, 18" x 18".

Carol Signett, Ferndale, Washington, 16" x 20".

Muriel R. Pfaff, Marietta, Georgia, 20½" x 15".
Adaptation of a pattern by Kris Kerrigan.
Pattern was published in *American Patchwork
& Quilting*, September/October 2001.

Patriotic Quilts to Make

Make one for you and one for a friend! These Little Quilts are fun to make and will fill your home with patriotic spirit. Hang them on the wall, place one on a table, tuck another in a basket, and enjoy!

Countertop collectibles displayed with "Feedsack Flags," the doll quilt "Antique Churn Dash," and "Little Quilt Flags" take us back in time.

The patriotic theme is carried from room to room, with "Honor and Glory" displayed over a chair and "Checkerboard Stars" spread out on the table. As you enter the next room, other quilts await. "Hooray for the Red, White, and Blue" covers an antique toy box and "Stars and Stripes" creates visual excitement while hanging on the wall.

With a whimsical welcome, "Purple Mountain Majesties" and "Stitchery Sue Flag" greet visitors.

"Winter Spirit" is the backdrop for a collection of snowmen
certain to warm up those chilly days.

Powder rooms are a great place to show off special quilts and treasures. Antique children's dresses brighten the corner alongside "Homeland."

"Honor and Glory" hangs by a cupboard filled with quilts and collections. "Salute to Liberty" rests under a sailor's photo, and "Betsy's Best" provides color and balance on the cupboard back.

Be our guest! Layers of patchwork quilts, both old and new, dress the bed while "Celebration" hangs overhead.

A patriotic greeting awaits visitors. "Home of the Brave" is attached to the metal door with the help of magnets sewn to the back of the quilt. The ladder-back chair makes a wonderful display rack for Little Quilts. A basket nearby holds "Salute to Liberty."

Gather the red, white, and blue together for a cheerful breakfast area. "Stars and Stripes," "Betsy's Best," and "Homeland" are all on display. "Freedom Four Patch" rests under a bowl on the table.

Home of the Brave

By Alice Berg, 2001, Marietta, Georgia, 24½" x 24½".
A simple little house proudly displays the red, white, and blue.

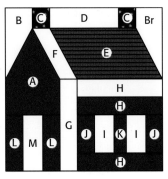

Templates: A, B, C, D, E, F, G, H, I, J, K, L, M, T, U, OO, PP

House Block
Finished size: 8"

MATERIALS

Yardage is based on 42"-wide fabric.

⭐ ⅝ yd. cream for house, house door, house windows, block background, block framing strips, and pieced border

⭐ ½ yd. red print for house front, house side, and second and pieced borders

⭐ 3" x 7" rectangle of blue stripe for house roof

⭐ 2" x 16" strip of blue print for house chimneys and first and second border corner squares

⭐ ½ yd. red-and-blue print for first and fourth borders

⭐ 1 yd. fabric for backing

⭐ ¼ yd. blue print for binding

⭐ 30" x 30" square of thin batting

⭐ Embroidery floss: red, blue, and gold

⭐ Template plastic

CUTTING

1. Using the patterns on page 89, make templates A, B, E, and F, whether you are hand or machine piecing. If you are hand piecing, refer to "Hand Piecing" on page 11 to make the tem-

plates. For machine piecing, trace the template patterns onto template plastic; follow the outer solid line on the patterns.

   If you are machine piecing, cut the pieces using the measurements given in the following steps. Also cut the template pieces that are not shown in parentheses—A, B, E, and F. For hand piecing, cut all of the template pieces listed. Make sure to mark the pivot points on the wrong side of each piece cut with a template.

2. From the cream fabric, cut:
   • 1 strip (template M), 1½" x 3¼", for house door
   • 2 rectangles (template I), 1½" x 2⅜", for house windows
   • 1 strip (template G), 1⅜" x 5", for house
   • 1 strip (template H), 1⅜" x 4⅞", for house
   • 1 strip (template D), 1½" x 4", for block background
   • 1 of template F for house
   • 1 of template B for block background
   • 1 of template B reversed for block background
   • 16 rectangles, 2½" x 4½", or 16 triangles (template OO), for pieced border

3. From the red print, cut:
   • 1 of template A for house front
   • 2 strips (template L), 1⅜" x 3¼", for house front
   • 2 strips (template H), 1⅜" x 4⅞", for house side
   • 2 rectangles (template J), 1⅜" x 2⅜", for house side
   • 1 strip (template K), 1⅛" x 2⅜", for house side
   • 32 squares, 2½" x 2½", or 32 triangles (template T), for pieced border
   • 4 squares (template U), 2½" x 2½", for pieced border corner squares

4. From the blue stripe, cut 1 of template E for house roof.

5. From the blue print, cut:
   • 2 rectangles (template C), 1⅜" x 1½", for house chimneys
   • 8 squares (template PP), 1½" x 1½", for first and second border corner squares

QUILT-TOP ASSEMBLY

1. Arrange the block pieces, and machine- or hand-sew them together into sections as shown. Sew the sections together. Stitch the template B pieces to the block last, pivoting at the seam intersections.

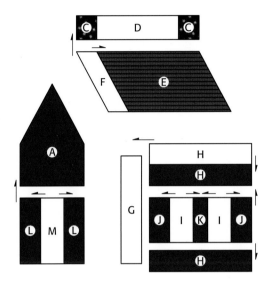

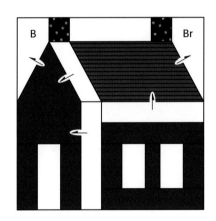

2. To make the block framing strips, measure the block as described in "Adding Borders" on page 14. Cut 2½"-wide strips from the cream fabric to the lengths measured, and stitch them to the quilt top. Press the seams toward the framing strips.

3. Referring to the photo for placement, transfer the flag embroidery pattern on page 38 to the house front. Refer to "Embroidering" on page 13 to stem stitch the stripes with red floss, the outline of the flag star field with blue floss, and the flagpole with gold floss. Cross-stitch the stars with blue floss.

4. For the first border, measure the quilt top as described in "Adding Borders" on page 14. Measure for the side *and* top and bottom borders. From the red-and-blue print fabric, cut 2 strips, each 1½" wide by the length measured; and 2 strips, 1½" wide by the width measured. Stitch the side borders to the sides of the quilt top. Press the seams toward the borders. Stitch a 1½" blue print border corner square (template PP) to the ends of the remaining 2 strips. Stitch the pieced border strips to the top and bottom edges of the quilt top. Press the seams toward the borders.

5. Repeat step 4 to add the second border, cutting 1½"-wide border strips from the red print fabric.

6. Now make the pieced border. If you rotary cut the pieces, refer to "Flying Geese" on page 18 to make 16 flying-geese units; use the 2½" x 4½" cream rectangles and the 2½" x 2½" red print squares. If you cut the pieces with templates, sew small triangles (template T) to each short side of each large triangle (template OO). Make 16 flying-geese units.

Make 16.

7. Sew 4 flying-geese units together as shown. Make 4 strips.

Make 4.

8. Sew 2 pieced border strips to the sides of the quilt top, placing the cream portion of the strips closest to the second border. Press the seams toward the borders. Stitch a red print 2½" x 2½" square (template U) to each end of the remaining pieced border strips. Sew the strips to the top and bottom edges of the quilt top. Press the seams toward the borders.

9. For the fourth border, refer to "Adding Borders" on page 14 to measure the quilt top for borders. Cut 2½"-wide strips from the red-and-blue print fabric to the lengths measured and sew them to the quilt top. Press the seams toward the borders.

QUILT FINISHING

Refer to "Quilt Finishing" on pages 14–16.

1. Layer the quilt top with batting and backing; baste.
2. Quilt as desired.
3. Bind the edges of the quilt.
4. Tea dye if desired.
5. Press the quilt.

Quilting Suggestion

Quilt in the ditch of all the pieces.

Home of the Brave
Embroidery Pattern

Homeland

By Alice Berg and Mary Ellen Von Holt, 2001, Marietta, Georgia, 17½" x 23½".
This neighborhood is all dressed up for a patriotic celebration.

Templates: P, Q, Z, BB, CC, DD, EE, FF, GG, HH, II, KK

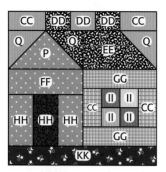

House Block
Finished size: 6"

Border Flag Block
Finished size: 2½" x 6"

MATERIALS

Yardage is based on 42"-wide fabric.

⭐ 2½" x 9" strip from *each* of 6 assorted sky fabrics

⭐ 2½" x 11" strip from *each* of 6 assorted chimney and roof fabrics

⭐ 4" x 7" rectangle from *each* of 6 assorted house front fabrics

⭐ 2" x 3" rectangle from *each* of 6 assorted door fabrics

⭐ 1½" x 6" strip from *each* of 6 assorted window fabrics

⭐ 1½" x 12" strip from *each* of 6 assorted house body fabrics

⭐ 1½" x 7" strip from *each* of 6 assorted grass fabrics

⭐ ¼ yd. red solid for flag stripes

⭐ ⅛ yd. white solid for flag stripes

⭐ ¼ yd. blue print for flag star fields

⭐ 3½" x 13" strip of gold print for border corner squares

⭐ ¾ yd. fabric for backing

⭐ ¼ yd. blue print for binding

⭐ 23" x 29" piece of thin batting

CUTTING

The following steps list rotary cutting measurements. Template letters for hand piecing are shown in parentheses.

1. From *each* of the 6 assorted sky strips, cut:
   • 2 rectangles (template CC), 1¼" x 2"
   • 1 rectangle (template DD), 1¼" x 1½"
   • 2 squares, 2" x 2", or 2 small triangles (template Q)
2. From *each* of the 6 assorted roof and chimney strips, cut:
   • 2 rectangles (template DD), 1¼" x 1½"
   • 1 rectangle, 2" x 3½", or 1 rectangle with cut corner (template EE)
   • 1 square, 2" x 2", or 1 small triangle (template Q)
3. From *each* of the 6 house front rectangles, cut:
   • 2 rectangles (template HH), 1½" x 2½"
   • 1 rectangle (template FF), 1½" x 3½"
   • 1 rectangle, 2" x 3½", or 1 large triangle (template P)
4. From *each* of the 6 door rectangles, cut 1 rectangle (template HH), 1½" x 2½".
5. From *each* of the 6 window strips, cut 4 squares (template II), 1¼" x 1¼".
6. From *each* of the 6 house body strips, cut:
   • 2 rectangles (template GG), 1¼" x 3½"
   • 2 rectangles (template CC), 1¼" x 2"
7. From *each* of the 6 grass strips, cut 1 strip (template KK), 1¼" x 6½".
8. From the red solid, cut 30 strips (template Z), 1" x 4", for flag stripes.
9. From the white solid, cut 20 strips (template Z), 1" x 4", for flag stripes.
10. From the blue print, cut 10 squares (template BB), 3" x 3", for flag star fields.
11. From the gold print, cut 4 squares (template BB), 3" x 3", for border corner squares.

QUILT-TOP ASSEMBLY

1. To make the House blocks, refer to "Flying Geese" on page 18. Stitch 2" x 2" sky and roof squares to the sides of the 2" x 3½" house front rectangles as shown. Make 6. Sew 2" matching sky squares to the right-hand side of the 2" x 3½" roof rectangles. Make 6.

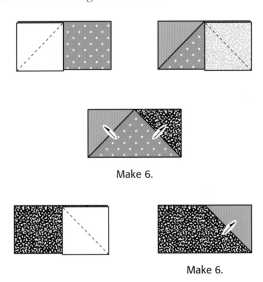

Make 6.

Make 6.

If you used templates, sew sky and roof triangles (template Q) to the short side of each large triangle (template P). Make 6. Sew small sky triangles (template Q) to the right-hand side of each template EE piece. Make 6.

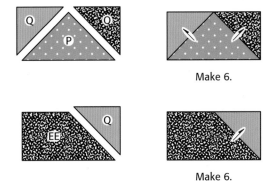

Make 6.

Make 6.

2. Arrange the block pieces as shown, making sure the fabric pieces for the house front, house side, roof, and sky match in each block. Machine-sew or hand-sew the pieces together into sections as shown. Sew the sections together. Make 6 House blocks.

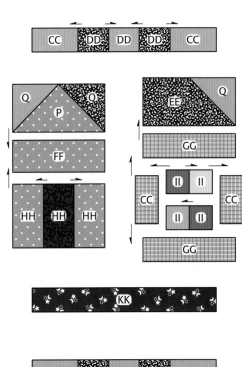

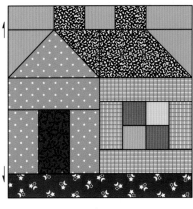

Make 6.

3. To make the Border Flag blocks, alternately sew together 3 red and 2 white 1" x 4" strips (template Z) as shown. Press the seams toward the red strips. Make 10 pieced rectangles. Stitch a 3" x 3" blue square (template BB) to

one short side of each pieced rectangle. Make 10 Border Flag blocks.

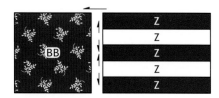

Make 6.

4. Arrange the House blocks, Border Flag blocks, and gold border corner squares (template BB) as shown. Stitch the pieces together into rows. Press the seams in alternate directions from row to row. Stitch the rows together.

QUILT FINISHING

Refer to "Quilt Finishing" on pages 14–16.

1. Layer the quilt top with batting and backing; baste.
2. Quilt as desired.
3. Bind the edges of the quilt.
4. Tea dye if desired.
5. Press the quilt.

Refer to "Quilt Finishing" on pages 14–16.

Quilting Suggestion

Quilt in the ditch. Quilt a wavy line through the border flag stripes.

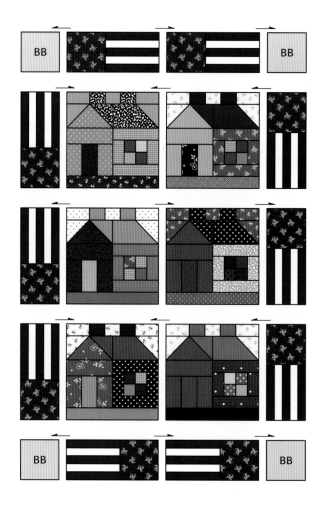

Feedsack Flags

By Alice Berg, 2001, Marietta, Georgia, 21¼" x 25".
Red reproduction fabrics are quickly sewn into Log Cabin–style flags.

Log Cabin Flag Block
Finished size: 3"

MATERIALS

Yardage is based on 42"-wide fabric.

⭐ ⅛ yd. dark blue pin-dot for flag star fields

⭐ ¼ yd. *total* assorted red prints for body of flags

⭐ ⅜ yd. medium blue print for sashing and inner border

⭐ ⅜ yd. red solid for middle border and binding

⭐ ⅜ yd. light blue print for outer border

⭐ 1 yd. fabric for backing

⭐ 26" x 30" rectangle of thin batting

CUTTING

The following steps list rotary cutting measurements. When available, template letters for hand piecing are shown in parentheses; some pieces are quite large and would require template patterns in sizes too big to fit in the book.

1. From the dark blue pin-dot, cut 20 squares (template O), 2" x 2", for flag star fields.
2. From the assorted red prints, cut 20 matching sets of 1 square (template O), 2" x 2", and 1 rectangle (template R), 2" x 3½", for body of flags.
3. From the medium blue print, cut:
   - 15 strips (template GG), 1¼" x 3½", for vertical sashing strips
   - 4 strips, 1¼" x 14¾", for horizontal sashing strips

QUILT-TOP ASSEMBLY

1. Stitch each 2" x 2" blue pin-dot square (template O) to a 2" x 2" assorted red print square (template O). Sew a matching 2" x 3½" assorted red print rectangle (template R) to the bottom of the pieced squares. Press the seams in the directions indicated. Make 20 Log Cabin Flag blocks.

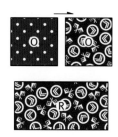
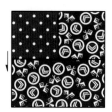

2. Arrange the blocks and sashing strips as shown. Stitch the blocks and vertical sashing strips together into rows. Press the seams toward the sashing strips. Stitch the block rows and horizontal sashing strips together. Press the seams toward the horizontal sashing strips.

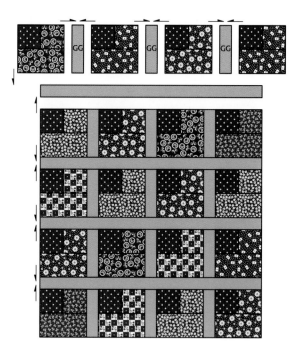

3. Measure the quilt top for borders as described in "Adding Borders" on page 14. For the inner border, cut 1¼"-wide strips from the medium blue fabric to the lengths measured and stitch them to the quilt top. For the middle border, cut 1"-wide strips from the red solid to the lengths measured and stitch them to the quilt top. For the outer border, cut 2½"-wide strips from the light blue fabric to the lengths measured and stitch them to the quilt top. Press the seams toward the border strip after each addition.

QUILT FINISHING

Refer to "Quilt Finishing" on pages 14–16.

1. Layer the quilt top with batting and backing; baste.
2. Quilt as desired.
3. Bind the edges of the quilt.
4. Tea dye if desired.
5. Press the quilt.

Quilting Suggestion

Quilt in the ditch around the flags and middle border. Quilt through the center of the sashing strips with a straight line, and quilt a wavy line in the outer border.

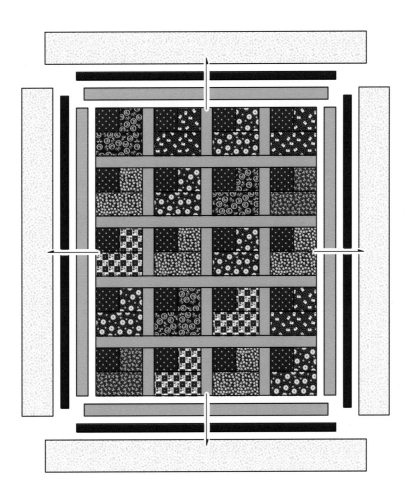

Winter Spirit

By Alice Berg and Wanda Hizer, 2001, Marietta, Georgia, 19" x 25".
Our snowman may be chilly on the outside, but his spirit is warm on the inside.

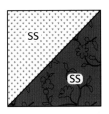 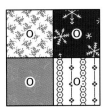

Templates: O, SS

Half-Square-Triangle Block
Finished size: 3"

Four Patch Block
Finished size: 3"

MATERIALS

Yardage is based on 42"-wide fabric.

⭐ ⅜ yd. *total* assorted light prints for blocks

⭐ ⅜ yd. *total* assorted blue prints for blocks

⭐ ¼ yd. dark blue for inner border

⭐ ¼ yd. blue plaid for outer border

⭐ 4" x 7" scrap of white-on-white print for snowman appliqué

⭐ 2" x 3" scrap of black solid for hat appliqué

⭐ 2" x 3" scrap of red stripe for flag appliqué

⭐ 1½" x 2" scrap of blue print for flag star field appliqué

⭐ Embroidery floss: brown, gold, and black

⭐ ⅞ yd. fabric for backing

⭐ ¼ yd. blue print for binding

⭐ 24" x 30" rectangle of thin batting

⭐ Buttons: 2 yellow stars; assorted white, blue, and black

⭐ Paper-backed fusible web (optional)

ROTARY CUTTING AND MACHINE PIECING

If you prefer to hand piece, see "Template Cutting and Hand Piecing" below.

1. From the light print fabrics for blocks, cut a total of 6 squares, each 3⅞" x 3⅞". From the blue prints for blocks, cut a total of six 3⅞" x 3⅞" squares. Cut each light and blue square once diagonally to yield 12 light print triangles and 12 blue print triangles. Stitch each light print triangle to a blue print triangle to make 12 Half-Square-Triangle blocks.

2. Cut the remainder of the light print and blue print fabrics for blocks into 2"-wide strips. Refer to "Four Patch Blocks" on page 17. Randomly stitch a light print strip to a blue print strip. Crosscut the strips into 24 segments, each 2" wide. Stitch 2 segments together to make 1 Four Patch block. Repeat to make a total of 12 Four Patch blocks.

TEMPLATE CUTTING AND HAND PIECING

Use templates O and SS on pages 90 and 96.

1. Cut a total of 6 triangles (template SS) from the light print fabrics for blocks. Cut a total of 6 triangles (template SS) from the blue print fabrics for blocks. Stitch each light print triangle to a blue print triangle to make 12 Half-Square-Triangle blocks.

Make 12.

2. From the remaining light print fabrics for blocks, cut a total of 24 squares (template O). From the remaining blue print fabrics for blocks, cut a total of 24 squares (template O). Stitch 2 light print squares and 2 blue print squares together as shown to make 12 Four Patch blocks.

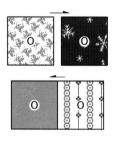

Make 12.

QUILT-TOP ASSEMBLY

1. Alternately arrange the blocks into rows as shown. Stitch the blocks in each row together. Press the seams toward the Half-Square-Triangle blocks. Stitch the rows together.

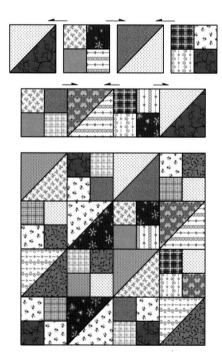

2. Measure the quilt top for borders as described in "Adding Borders" on page 14. For the inner border, cut 1¼"-wide strips from the dark blue fabric to the lengths measured and stitch them to the quilt top. For the outer border, cut 3"-wide strips from the blue plaid to the lengths measured and stitch them to the quilt top. After each addition, press the seams toward the newly sewn border strips.

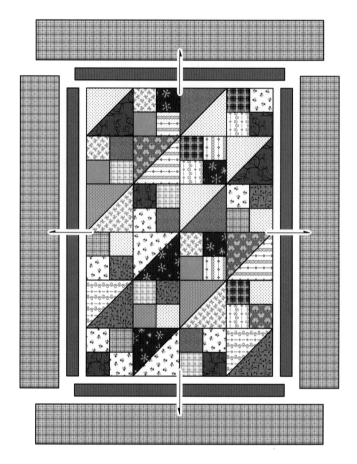

3. Refer to "Appliquéing" on page 12 to cut the appliqué pieces on page 49 from the fabrics indicated. Cut one of each piece.

4. Referring to the photo for placement, appliqué the snowman and flag shapes to the lower left corner of the quilt top in the numerical order indicated. Use your favorite appliqué method.

5. Refer to "Embroidering" on page 13 to stem stitch the snowman arms with brown embroidery floss and the flagpole with gold embroidery floss. Use black floss to make French knots for the eyes and mouth.

QUILT FINISHING

Refer to "Quilt Finishing" on pages 14–16.

1. Layer the quilt top with batting and backing; baste.
2. Quilt as desired.
3. Bind the edges of the quilt.
4. Tea dye if desired.
5. Refer to the photo and the diagram below to stitch the buttons to the quilt top.
6. Press the quilt.

Quilting Suggestion

Quilt through the center of the Four Patch blocks in an **X**. Quilt in the ditch of the Half-Square-Triangle blocks and inner border. Quilt the outer border with curls that look like wind blowing.

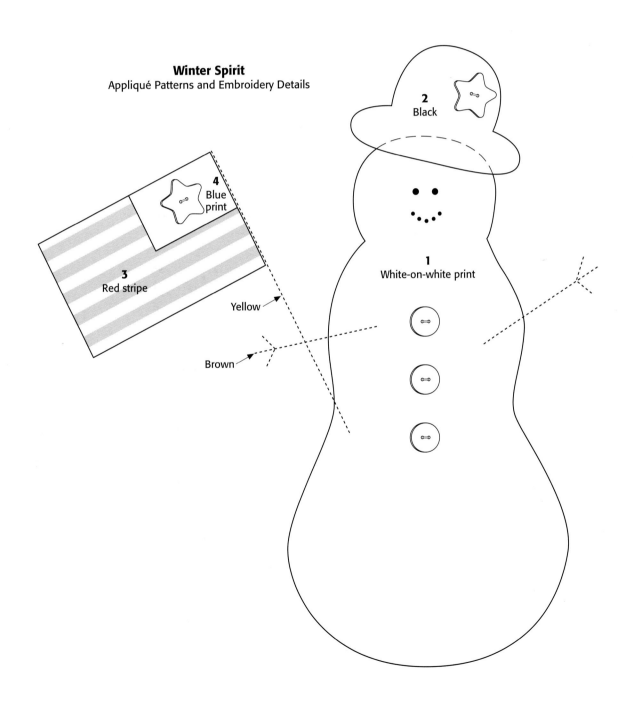

Winter Spirit
Appliqué Patterns and Embroidery Details

2 Black

1 White-on-white print

4 Blue print

3 Red stripe

Yellow

Brown

Stars and Stripes

By Mary Ellen Von Holt, 2001, Marietta, Georgia, 24½" x 30½".
"Whose broad stripes and bright stars…"
—from "The Star-Spangled Banner" by Francis Scott Key

Templates: O, P, Q, S, T

Sawtooth Star Block
Finished size: 6"

MATERIALS
Yardage is based on 42"-wide fabric.

⭐ ⅝ yd. *total* assorted color prints for block stars

⭐ ⅝ yd. *total* assorted light prints for block backgrounds

⭐ ¼ yd. gold print for inner border

⭐ ¼ yd. light print for outer pieced border

⭐ ¼ yd. *total* assorted red prints for outer pieced border

⭐ 1 yd. fabric for backing

⭐ ¼ yd. blue print for binding

⭐ 30" x 36" rectangle of thin batting

CUTTING
The following steps list rotary cutting measurements. Template letters for hand piecing are shown in parentheses.

1. From the assorted color prints, cut:
   - 12 squares (template S), 3½" x 3½", for block centers
   - 12 sets of 8 matching squares (96 total), 2" x 2", or 12 sets of 8 matching small triangles (template Q), for flying-geese units

2. From the assorted light prints, cut:
   - 12 sets of 4 matching rectangles (48 total), 2" x 3½", or 4 triangles (template P), for flying-geese units
   - 12 sets of 4 squares (template O) (48 total), 2" x 2", for block corners

3. From the light print for the outer pieced border, cut a total of twenty-five 2⅞" x 2⅞" squares. From the assorted red prints for the outer pieced border, cut a total of twenty-five 2⅞" x 2⅞" squares. Cut each square once diagonally to yield 50 light print triangles and 50 assorted red print triangles (template T) for the outer pieced border.

QUILT-TOP ASSEMBLY

1. Refer to "Flying Geese" on page 18 to use the 2" x 3½" light print rectangles and the 2" x 2" assorted color squares to make 12 sets of 4 matching flying-geese units. If you used templates, sew small triangles (template Q) to each short side of each large triangle (template P).

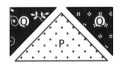 

Make 12 sets of
4 matching units.

2. Stitch 4 flying-geese units, 1 block center (template S), and 4 corner squares (template O) together as shown. You can choose to use identical pieces for each unit of the block or mix the fabrics to create a scrappy look (refer to "Make It Scrappy" on page 19). Make 12 Sawtooth Star blocks.

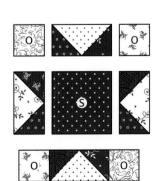 

Make 12.

3. Arrange the quilt blocks as desired into 4 horizontal rows of 3 blocks each. Stitch the blocks in each row together. Press the seams in opposite directions from row to row. Stitch the rows together.

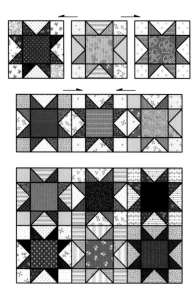

4. Measure the quilt top for borders as described in "Adding Borders" on page 14. For the inner border, cut 1½"-wide inner border strips from the gold print to the lengths measured and stitch them to the quilt top. Press the seams toward the borders.

5. Stitch each light print triangle (template T) to an assorted red print triangle (template T). Make 50 half-square-triangle units.

Make 50.

6. Join 13 half-square-triangle units together as shown for the side borders. Make 2. Join 12 half-square-triangle units together as shown for the top and bottom borders. Make 2.

Top and Bottom Border
Make 2.

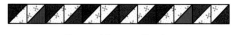

Side Border
Make 2.

7. Stitch the side borders to the sides of the quilt top as shown. Press the seams toward the borders. Stitch the top and bottom borders to the top and bottom edges of the quilt top as shown. Press the seams toward the borders.

QUILT FINISHING

Refer to "Quilt Finishing" on pages 14–16.

1. Layer the quilt top with batting and backing; baste.
2. Quilt as desired.
3. Bind the edges of the quilt.
4. Tea dye if desired.
5. Press the quilt.

Quilting Suggestion

Quilt diagonal lines in the center square of the Sawtooth Star blocks. Outline quilt in the block backgrounds. Quilt wavy lines in the red stripes of the pieced border.

Freedom Four Patch

By Alice Berg and Libby Lowe, 2001, Marietta, Georgia, 20¼" x 24½".
Stitch up a patchwork celebration with this simple Little Quilt.
Quilts like this one are great to display with collectibles.

Templates: O, N, S, X

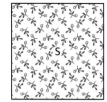

Four Patch Block
Finished size: 3"

Plain Block
Finished size: 3"

MATERIALS

Yardage is based on 42"-wide fabric.

⭐ ¼ yd. *total* assorted prints for Four Patch blocks

⭐ ⅜ yd. *total* assorted blue prints for plain blocks and setting triangles

⭐ ¼ yd. red print for inner border

⭐ ¼ yd. blue stripe for outer border sides

⭐ ¼ yd. blue print for top and bottom of outer border

⭐ ⅞ yd. fabric for backing

⭐ ¼ yd. red solid for binding

⭐ 24" x 28" rectangle of thin batting

ROTARY CUTTING AND MACHINE PIECING

If you prefer to hand piece, see "Template Cutting and Hand Piecing" below.

1. From the assorted prints for blocks, cut 2"-wide strips. Refer to "Four Patch Blocks" on page 17 to randomly stitch 2 strips together. Crosscut the strips into 24 segments, each 2" wide. Stitch 2 segments together. Make 12 Four Patch blocks.

2. From the assorted blue prints, cut:
   - 6 squares, 3½" x 3½", for plain blocks
   - 3 squares, 5½" x 5½". Cut each square twice diagonally to yield 12 side setting triangles. You will use 10 and have 2 left over.
   - 2 squares, 3" x 3". Cut each square once diagonally to yield 4 corner setting triangles.

TEMPLATE CUTTING AND HAND PIECING

Use templates O, N, S, and X on pages 90, 91, and 92.

1. From the assorted prints for blocks, cut 48 squares (template O). Stitch 4 squares together as shown to make 12 Four Patch blocks.

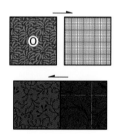

Make 12.

2. From the assorted blue prints, cut:
   - 6 squares (template S), for plain blocks
   - 10 triangles (template N), for side setting triangles
   - 4 triangles (template X), for corner setting triangles

QUILT-TOP ASSEMBLY

1. Arrange the Four Patch blocks, plain blocks, and setting triangles into diagonal rows as shown, adding the top and bottom corner triangles last.

2. Measure the quilt top for borders as described in "Adding Borders" on page 14. For the inner border, cut 1½"-wide strips from the red print fabric to the length measured and stitch them to the quilt top. For the outer side borders, cut 3"-wide strips from the blue stripe to the length measured and stitch them to the quilt sides. For the outer top and bottom borders, cut 3"-wide strips from the blue print to the length measured; stitch them to the quilt top and bottom edges. After each addition, press the seams toward the newly sewn border strips.

QUILT FINISHING

Refer to "Quilt Finishing" on pages 14–16.

1. Layer the quilt top with batting and backing; baste.
2. Quilt as desired.
3. Bind the edges of the quilt.
4. Tea dye if desired.
5. Press the quilt.

Quilting Suggestion

Quilt your project with cross-hatching that goes through the center of the Four Patch blocks and extends into the borders.

Purple Mountain Majesties

By Alice Berg and Libby Lowe, 2001, Marietta, Georgia, 25½" x 25½".
Lyrics from patriotic songs can inspire a quilt. The words from the song
"America the Beautiful" were the inspiration for this quilt.

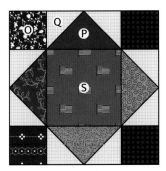

Templates: O, P, Q, S, PP

Square-in-a-Square Block
Finished size: 6"

MATERIALS

Yardage is based on 42"-wide fabric.

⭐ ½ yd. *total* assorted purple prints for block centers

⭐ ½ yd. *total* assorted gold prints for block background and sashing

⭐ ¼ yd. *total* assorted red prints for block corners

⭐ ½ yd. purple for sashing squares and border

⭐ 1 yd. fabric for backing

⭐ ¼ yd. red print for binding

⭐ 30" x 30" square of thin batting

CUTTING

The following steps list rotary cutting measurements. When available, template letters for hand piecing are shown in parentheses; some pieces are quite large and would require template patterns in sizes too big to fit in the book.

1. From one of the assorted purple prints, cut 9 squares (template S), 3½" x 3½", for block centers.

2. From the remaining assorted purple prints, cut a *total* of 36 rectangles, 2" x 3½", or 36 large triangles (template P), for flying-geese units.

3. From the assorted gold prints, cut a *total* of:
   • 9 sets of 8 matching squares (72 total), 2" x 2", or cut 72 small triangles (template Q), for flying-geese units
   • 12 strips, 1½" x 6½", for sashing

4. From the assorted red prints, cut a *total* of 36 squares (template O), 2" x 2", for block corners.

5. From the purple for sashing squares and border, cut 4 squares (template PP), 1½" x 1½", for sashing squares.

QUILT-TOP ASSEMBLY

1. Refer to "Flying Geese" on page 18 to make 36 flying-geese units. Use the 2" x 3½" assorted purple print rectangles and matching gold 2" x 2" squares. If you used templates, sew small triangles (template Q) to each short side of each large triangle (template P).

Make 36.

2. Stitch together 1 purple block center (template S), 4 flying-geese units with matching gold prints, and 4 red corner squares (template O) as shown. Make 9 Square-in-a-Square blocks.

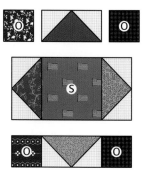
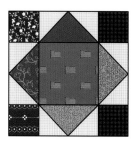

Make 9.

3. Arrange the blocks, sashing strips, and sashing squares (template PP) together as shown. Stitch the blocks and vertical sashing strips together to make the block rows. Press the seams toward the sashing strips. Stitch the horizontal sashing strips and sashing squares together to make the sashing rows. Press the seams toward the sashing strips. Stitch the block rows and sashing rows together.

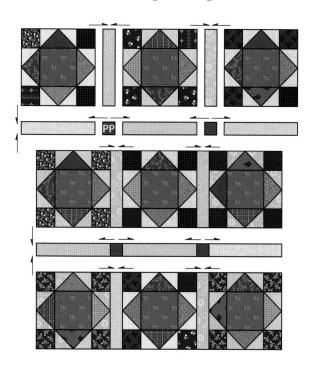

4. Measure the quilt top for borders as described in "Adding Borders" on page 14. Cut 3"-wide border strips from the purple border fabric to the lengths measured, and stitch them to the quilt-top edges. Press the seams toward the borders.

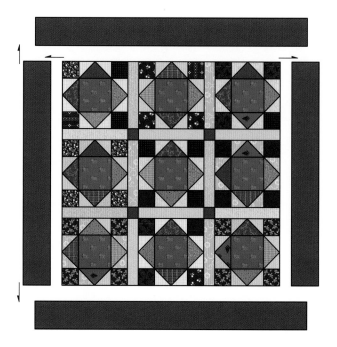

QUILT FINISHING
Refer to "Quilt Finishing" on pages 14–16.
1. Layer the quilt top with batting and backing; baste.
2. Quilt as desired.
3. Bind the edges of the quilt.
4. Tea dye if desired.
5. Press the quilt.

Quilting Suggestion
Quilt an **X** through the center of each block. Quilt 2 straight rows of stitches, side by side and 1" apart, in the outer border.

Betsy's Best

By Alice Berg and Wanda Hizer, 2001, Marietta, Georgia, 15½" x 10¼".
This Little Quilt is all dressed up and ready for hanging or framing.

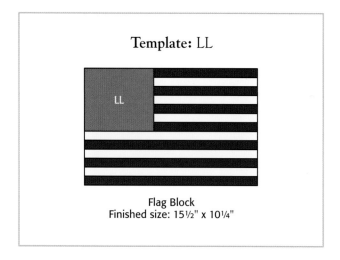

Template: LL

Flag Block
Finished size: 15½" x 10¼"

MATERIALS

Yardage is based on 42"-wide fabric.

⭐ 6" x 7" rectangle of blue solid for flag star field

⭐ ½ yd. red solid for stripes and binding

⭐ ¼ yd. white solid for stripes

⭐ 3" x 6" rectangle from *each* of 2 assorted gold prints for star appliqués

⭐ 4" x 8" rectangle of red print for flower appliqués

⭐ 3" x 3" piece of yellow check for flower center appliqués

⭐ 4" x 12" piece of green print for leaf and stem appliqués

⭐ ⅝ yd. fabric for backing

⭐ 15" x 20" piece of thin batting

⭐ Paper-backed fusible web (optional)

CUTTING

The following steps list rotary cutting measurements. When available, template letters for hand piecing are shown in parentheses; some pieces are quite large and would require template patterns in sizes too big to fit in the book.

1. From the blue solid, cut 1 rectangle (template LL), 5¾" x 6½", for flag star field.
2. From the red solid, cut:
   - 4 strips, 1¼" x 9½", for upper stripes
   - 3 strips, 1¼" x 15½", for lower stripes
3. From the white solid, cut:
   - 3 strips, 1¼" x 9½", for upper stripes
   - 3 strips, 1¼" x 15½", for lower stripes

QUILT-TOP ASSEMBLY

1. Alternately stitch the 1¼" x 9½" red and white strips together along the long edges, beginning and ending with a red strip, to make the flag upper stripes. Repeat with the 1¼" x 15½" red and white strips, beginning with a white strip and ending with a red strip, to make the flag lower stripes.
2. Stitch the flag upper stripes, lower stripes, and blue solid rectangle together as shown.

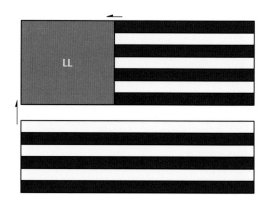

3. Refer to "Appliquéing" on page 12 to cut the appliqué pieces on page 61 from the fabrics indicated. Cut 1 long stem (template 1), 2 medium stems (template 2), 2 short stems (template 3), 4 leaves (template 4), 2 flowers (template 5), 2 flower centers (template 6), and 2 stars (template 7).

4. Referring to the photo for placement, appliqué the shapes to the flag block in the order indicated, using your favorite method.

QUILT FINISHING

Refer to "Quilt Finishing" on pages 14–16.

1. Layer the quilt top with batting and backing; baste.
2. Quilt as desired.
3. Bind the edges of the quilt.
4. Tea dye if desired.
5. Press the quilt.

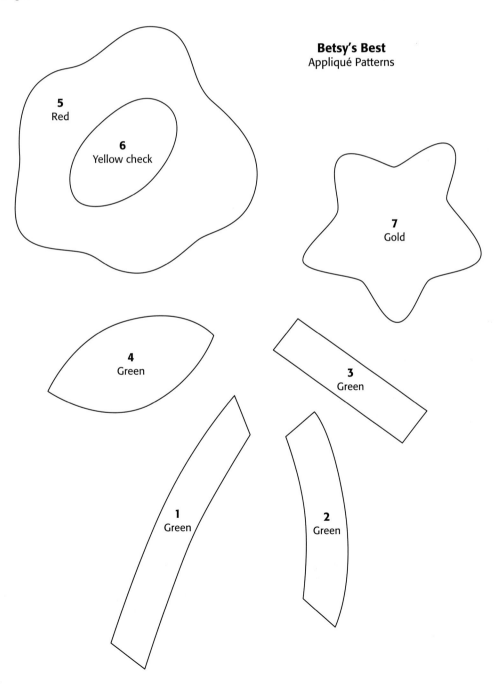

Betsy's Best
Appliqué Patterns

5
Red

6
Yellow check

7
Gold

4
Green

3
Green

1
Green

2
Green

Salute to Liberty

By Sylvia Johnson, 2001, Marietta, Georgia, 21½" x 24".
"The colors before us fly / But more than the flag is passing by"
— Henry Holcomb Bennett, "The Flag Goes By"

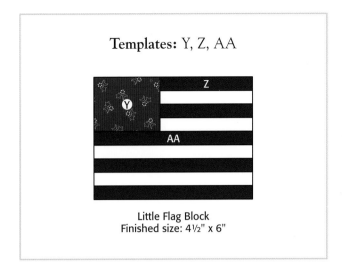

Templates: Y, Z, AA

Little Flag Block
Finished size: 4½" x 6"

MATERIALS

Yardage is based on 42"-wide fabric.

⭐ 3" x 10" strip from *each of 2 different blue prints for flag star fields*

⭐ ¼ yd. red solid for flag stripes

⭐ ¼ yd. white solid for flag stripes

⭐ ¼ yd. *total* assorted gold prints for sashing and inner border

⭐ ⅜ yd. red print for outer border

⭐ 1 yd. fabric for backing

⭐ ¼ yd. gold-and-red print for binding

⭐ 28" x 30" rectangle of thin batting

CUTTING

The following steps list rotary cutting measurements. When available, template letters for hand piecing are shown in parentheses; some pieces are quite large and would require template patterns in sizes too big to fit in the book.

1. From both of the 2 blue prints, cut 3 rectangles (template Y), 2½" x 3", for flag star fields.
2. From the red solid, cut:
   - 12 strips (template Z), 1" x 4", for flag upper stripes
   - 18 strips (template AA), 1" x 6½", for flag lower stripes

3. From the white solid, cut:
   - 12 strips (template Z), 1" x 4", for flag upper stripes
   - 12 strips (template AA), 1" x 6½", for flag lower stripes
4. From the assorted gold prints, cut a total of:
   - 4 strips, 1½" x 6½", for horizontal sashing strips
   - 3 strips, 1½" x 16", for vertical sashing strips

QUILT-TOP ASSEMBLY

1. Stitch 1 blue print rectangle (template Y), 2 red 1" x 4" strips (template Z), 2 white 1" x 4" strips (template Z), 3 red 1" x 6½" strips (template AA), and 2 white 1" x 6½" strips (template AA) together as shown. Make 6 Little Flag blocks.

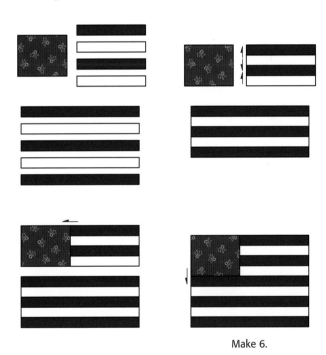

Make 6.

2. Arrange the blocks and sashing strips as shown. Stitch the blocks and horizontal sashing strips together into 2 vertical rows. Beginning and ending with a sashing strip, alternately stitch

the block rows and vertical sashing strips together.

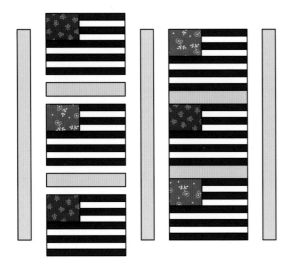

3. Referring to "Adding Borders" on page 14, cut 2 strips, each 1½" wide by the width of the quilt top, from the assorted gold print fabrics. Stitch the strips to the top and bottom edges of the quilt top to complete the inner border. Measure the quilt top for the outer borders. Cut 3½"-wide strips from the red print to the lengths measured and stitch them to the quilt top. After each addition, press the seams toward the newly sewn border strips.

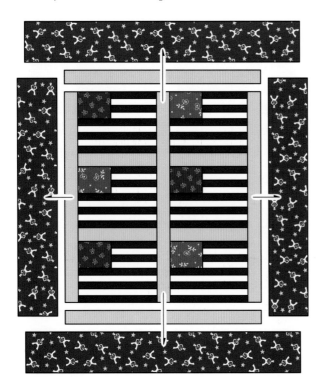

QUILT FINISHING

Refer to "Quilt Finishing" on pages 14–16.

1. Layer the quilt top with batting and backing; baste.
2. Quilt as desired.
3. Bind the edges of the quilt.
4. Tea dye if desired.
5. Press the quilt.

Quilting Suggestion

Quilt waves in the flag stripes. Quilt stars in the border and join them with wavy lines.

Flag Ornament

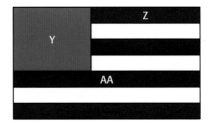

To make a small ornament, use the Little Flag block measurements on page 63 to cut 1 blue solid flag star field, 2 red and 2 white short stripes, and 2 red and 1 white long stripe. Layer the block with thin batting and backing fabric. Sew around the edges, leaving an opening for turning. Turn the ornament to the right side and slipstitch the opening closed. Sew a cord to the top for hanging. Use as an ornament or hang it from a doorknob or cupboard.

Antique Churn Dash

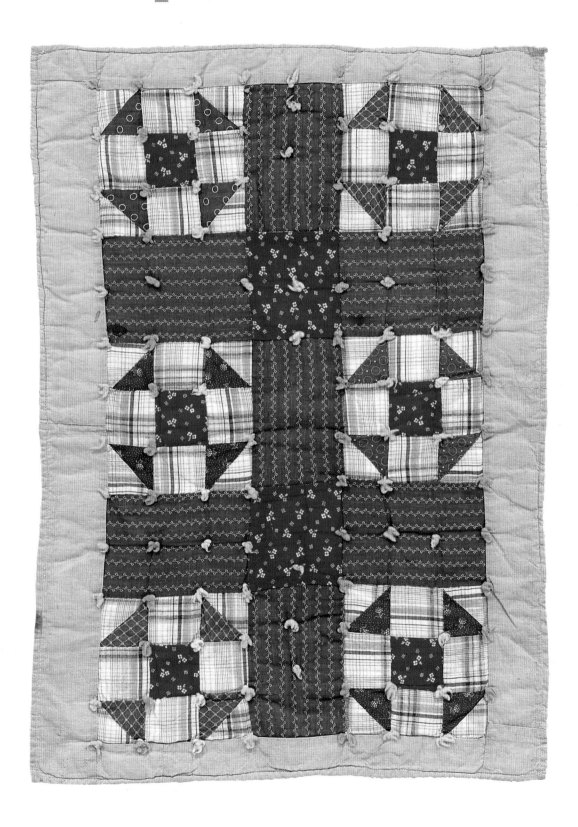

A well-worn antique doll quilt (18¼" x 26¾") adds a
wonderful patriotic touch to a country setting.

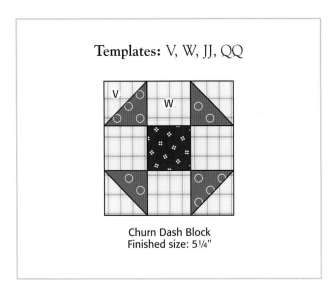

Templates: V, W, JJ, QQ

Churn Dash Block
Finished size: 5¼"

MATERIALS

Yardage is based on 42"-wide fabric.

⭐ ¼ yd. red print for block centers and sashing squares

⭐ ¼ yd. *total* assorted blue prints for blocks

⭐ ⅜ yd. light plaid for blocks

⭐ ¼ yd. blue print for sashing

⭐ ⅜ yd. light blue for border and binding

⭐ ⅞ yd. fabric for backing

⭐ 24" x 33" rectangle of thin batting

CUTTING

The following steps list rotary cutting measurements. Template letters for hand piecing are shown in parentheses.

1. From the red print, cut:
   - 6 squares (template W), 2¼" x 2¼", for block centers
   - 2 squares, 3¾" x 3¾" (template JJ), for sashing squares

2. From the assorted blue prints, cut 6 sets of 2 matching squares, each 2⅝" x 2⅝". Cut each square once diagonally to yield 6 sets of 4 matching triangles (template V) (24 total) for half-square-triangle units.

3. From the light plaid, cut:
   - 12 squares, 2⅝" x 2⅝". Cut each square once diagonally to yield 24 triangles (template V) for half-square-triangle units.
   - 24 squares (template W), 2¼" x 2¼", for blocks

4. From the blue print for sashing, cut 7 strips (template QQ), 3¾" x 5¾".

QUILT-TOP ASSEMBLY

1. Join each blue triangle (template V) to a light plaid triangle (template V). Make 24 half-square-triangle units.

2. Stitch together 4 matching half-square-triangle units, 1 red block center (template W), and 4 light plaid squares (template W) as shown. Make 6 Churn Dash blocks.

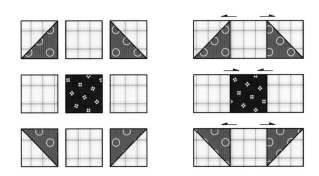

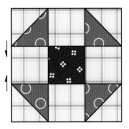

Make 6.

3. Arrange the blocks, sashing strips (template QQ), and sashing squares (template JJ) as shown. Stitch the pieces together into rows. Stitch the rows together. Press seams in opposite directions from row to row.

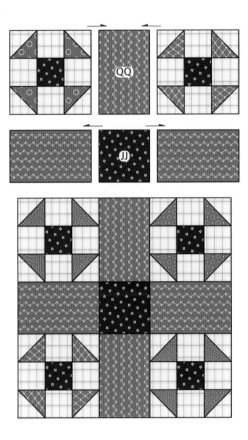

4. Measure the quilt top for borders as described in "Adding Borders" on page 14. From the light blue border fabric, cut 1¾"-wide strips to the lengths measured and stitch them to the quilt top.

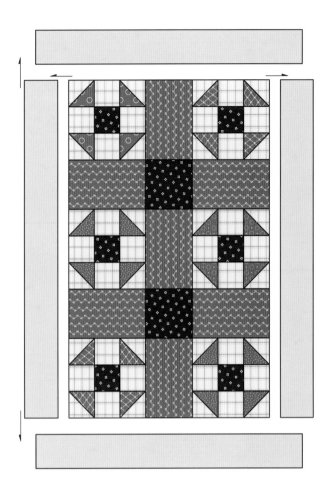

QUILT FINISHING

Refer to "Quilt Finishing" on pages 14–16.

1. Layer the quilt top with batting and backing; baste.
2. Quilt as desired.
3. Bind the edges of the quilt.
4. Tea dye if desired.
5. Press the quilt.

Quilting Suggestion

Tie the layers together with embroidery floss or yarn.

Hooray for the
Red, White, and Blue

By Sylvia Johnson, 2001, Marietta, Georgia, 20" x 20".
Pinwheels twirl in the air as the parade passes by!

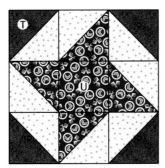

Templates: S, T, U

Friendship Star Block
Finished size: 6"

MATERIALS

Yardage is based on 42"-wide fabric.

⭐ 3" x 7" strip from *each* of 4 assorted blue prints for block corners

⭐ 3" x 9" strip from *each* of 4 assorted red prints for stars

⭐ ¼ yd. light print for block backgrounds

⭐ ¼ yd. gold print for inner border

⭐ ¼ yd. red solid for outer border

⭐ ¼ yd. white solid for outer border

⭐ ¼ yd. dark blue print for border corners and binding

⭐ 3" x 12" scrap of dark gold print for star appliqués

⭐ ⅞ yd. fabric for backing

⭐ 25" x 25" square of thin batting

⭐ Paper-backed fusible web (optional)

CUTTING

The following steps list rotary cutting measurements. When available, template letters for hand piecing are shown in parentheses; some pieces are quite large and would require template patterns in sizes too big to fit in the book.

1. From *each* of the 4 assorted red prints, cut:
   • 1 square (template U), 2½" x 2½", for star center
   • 2 squares, 2⅞" x 2⅞". Cut each square once diagonally to yield 4 triangles (template T) for the half-square-triangle units.

2. From *each* of the 4 assorted blue prints, cut 2 squares, 2⅞" x 2⅞". Cut each square once diagonally to yield 4 triangles (template T) for the half-square-triangle units.

3. From the light print, cut 16 squares, 2⅞" x 2⅞". Cut each square once diagonally to yield 32 triangles (template T) for the half-square-triangle units.

4. From the red solid, cut four 1½" x 42" strips for the outer border strip set.

5. From the white solid, cut two 1½" x 42" strips for the outer border strip set.

6. From the dark blue print, cut 4 squares (template S), 3½" x 3½", for the outer border corners.

QUILT-TOP ASSEMBLY

1. Stitch each blue print triangle and red print triangle (template T) to a light print triangle (template T). Make 16 blue and 16 red half-square-triangle units.

2. Stitch 4 matching blue half-square-triangle units, 4 matching red half-square-triangle units, and 1 matching star center (template U) as shown. Make 4 Friendship Star blocks.

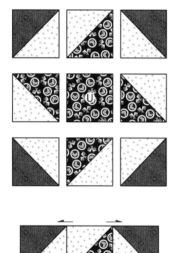

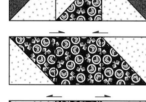

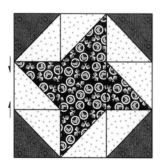

3. Arrange the blocks as shown. Stitch the blocks together into rows. Press the seams in opposite directions. Stitch the rows together.

4. Measure the quilt top for borders as described in "Adding Borders" on page 14. For the inner border, cut 1¼"-wide strips from the gold print to the lengths measured and stitch them to the quilt-top edges.

5. For the outer border, stitch a red 1½" x 42" strip to each side of a white 1½" x 42" strip to make a strip set. Make 2. Measure the length and width of the quilt top through the horizontal and vertical centers. From the strip sets, cut 2 strips to the length measured and stitch them to the quilt sides. Cut 2 strips to the width measured. Refer to "Appliquéing" on page 12 to cut 4 star shapes from the dark gold print, using the pattern at right. Center 1 star on each 3½" dark blue square (template S) and appliqué it in place with your favorite method. Sew an appliquéd square to the ends of each strip. Stitch the pieced border strips to the top and bottom edges of the quilt top. After each addition, press the seams toward the newly sewn border strips.

QUILT FINISHING

Refer to "Quilt Finishing" on pages 14–16.

1. Layer the quilt top with batting and backing; baste.
2. Quilt as desired.
3. Bind the edges of the quilt.
4. Tea dye if desired.
5. Press the quilt.

Quilting Suggestion

Quilt in the ditch around the block stars, blue corner triangles, borders, and appliquéd stars.

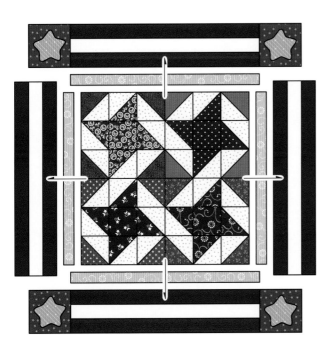

"Hooray for the Red, White, and Blue" and "Checkerboard Stars"
Appliqué Pattern

Checkerboard Stars

By Sylvia Johnson, 2001, Marietta, Georgia, 23" x 23".
This is a carry-along project. In no time at all, you'll have a whole galaxy of stars!

Template: S

Appliquéd Star Block
Finished size: 3"

Plain Block
Finished size: 3"

MATERIALS

Yardage is based on 42"-wide fabric.

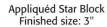 ¼ yd. cream print for star appliqués

🌟 ⅜ yd. blue print for appliquéd blocks

🌟 ½ yd. red print for plain blocks and binding

🌟 ¼ yd. cream print for inner border

🌟 ⅜ yd. blue print for outer border

🌟 ⅞ yd. fabric for backing

🌟 27" x 27" square of thin batting

🌟 Red embroidery floss

🌟 Paper-backed fusible web (optional)

CUTTING

The following steps list rotary cutting measurements. Template letters for hand piecing are shown in parentheses.

1. From the blue print, cut 13 squares (template S), 3½" x 3½", for appliquéd blocks.
2. From the red print, cut 12 squares (template S), 3½" x 3½", for plain blocks.

QUILT-TOP ASSEMBLY

1. Refer to "Appliquéing" on page 12 to cut 13 star shapes from the cream print fabric, using the pattern on page 71. Appliqué 1 star to each blue print square (template S) with your favorite method. Refer to "Embroidering" on page 13 to work a buttonhole stitch around each appliqué with red embroidery floss.
2. Arrange the appliquéd blocks and plain blocks as shown. Stitch the blocks in each row together. Press the seams toward the plain blocks. Stitch the rows together.

3. Measure the quilt top for borders as described in "Adding Borders" on page 14. For the inner border, cut 1¼"-wide strips from the cream print fabric to the lengths measured and stitch them to the quilt edges. Then cut 3½"-wide strips from the outer border blue print to the lengths measured and stitch them to the quilt edges. After each addition, press the seams toward the newly sewn border strips.

QUILT FINISHING
Refer to "Quilt Finishing" on pages 14–16.

1. Layer the quilt top with batting and backing; baste.
2. Quilt as desired.
3. Bind the edges of the quilt.
4. Tea dye if desired.
5. Press the quilt.

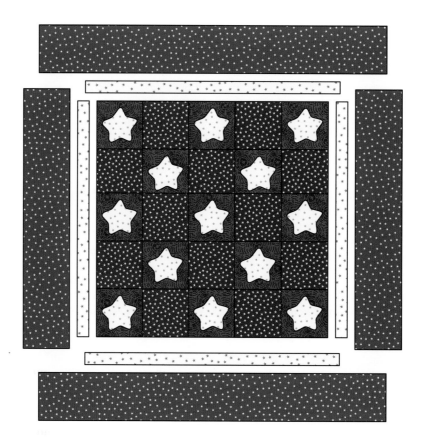

Honor and Glory

By Mary Ellen Von Holt and Mildred Moss, 2001, Marietta, Georgia, 34" x 46¾".
"...O'er the land of the free and the home of the brave"
—from "The Star-Spangled Banner" by Francis Scott Key.

Templates: N, P, Q, S, X, MM, NN

Flying Geese Block
Finished size: 1½" x 3"

Plain Block
Finished size: 6"

MATERIALS

Yardage is based on 42"-wide fabric.

⭐ ⅜ yd. *total* assorted red prints for Flying Geese blocks and sashing squares

⭐ ⅝ yd. *total* assorted blue prints for Flying Geese blocks and sashing squares

⭐ ⅝ yd. *total* assorted light prints for Flying Geese blocks

⭐ ½ yd. *total* assorted gold prints for plain blocks

⭐ ⅜ yd. gold print for large side setting triangles

⭐ ¼ yd. navy print for small side and corner setting triangles

⭐ ⅝ yd. red print for border

⭐ 1½ yds. fabric for backing

⭐ ⅜ yd. blue for binding

⭐ 38" x 51" rectangle of thin batting

CUTTING

The following steps list rotary cutting measurements. Template letters for hand piecing are shown in parentheses.

1. From the assorted red prints, cut:
   - 6 sets of 8 matching squares (48 total), 2" x 2", or 6 sets of 8 matching small triangles (template Q), for red flying-geese units
   - 6 squares (template S), 3½" x 3½", for sashing squares

2. From the assorted blue prints, cut:
   - 72 pairs of matching squares (144 total), 2" x 2", or 72 pairs of matching small triangles (template Q), for blue flying-geese units
   - 2 squares (template S), 3½" x 3½", for sashing squares

3. From the assorted light prints, cut 96 rectangles, 2" x 3½", or 96 large triangles (template P), for flying-geese units.

4. From the assorted gold prints, cut 7 squares (template MM), 6½" x 6½", for plain blocks.

5. From the gold print for large side setting triangles, cut 3 squares, 9¾" x 9¾". Cut each square twice diagonally to yield 12 triangles. You will use 10 and have 2 left over. Or, cut 10 triangles (template NN).

6. From the navy print, cut:
   - 2 squares, 3" x 3". Cut each square once diagonally to yield 4 corner setting triangles. Or, cut 4 triangles (template X).
   - 2 squares, 5½" x 5½". Cut each square twice diagonally to yield 8 small side setting triangles. You will use 6 and have 2 left over. Or, cut 6 triangles (template N).

QUILT-TOP ASSEMBLY

1. If you rotary cut the pieces, refer to "Flying Geese" on page 18 to use the matching pairs of red or blue 2" squares and light print rectangles to make 24 red and 72 blue Flying Geese blocks. If you used templates, sew matching small triangles (template Q) to each short side of each large triangle (template P).

 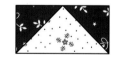

Make 24 red.
Make 72 blue.

2. Join 1 red and 3 blue flying-geese units to make a strip, making sure all units point the same way and that the red unit is at the top of the strip as shown. Make 24 strips.

3. Arrange the flying-geese strips, plain blocks (template MM), red and blue sashing squares (template S), small side setting triangles (template N), large side setting triangles (template NN), and corner setting triangles (template X) as shown. Sew the pieces together in diagonal rows. Press seams toward the plain blocks and setting triangles. Sew the rows together. Add the corner setting triangles last.

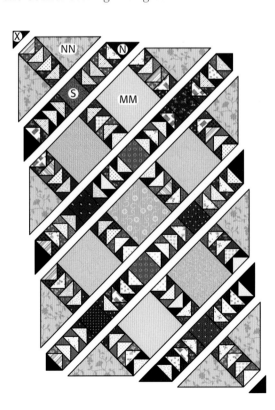

4. Measure the quilt top for borders as described in "Adding Borders" on page 14. From the red print for border, cut 4½"-wide strips to the lengths measured and stitch them to the quilt top.

QUILT FINISHING
Refer to "Quilt Finishing" on pages 14–16.
1. Layer the quilt top with batting and backing; baste.
2. Quilt as desired.
3. Bind the edges of the quilt.
4. Tea dye if desired.
5. Press the quilt.

Quilting Suggestion

Using variegated thread, free-motion quilt loops and stars all over the quilt.

Celebration

By Alice Berg, 1996, Marietta, Georgia, 40½" x 40½".
The eagle is a symbol of strength for the United States. This quilt,
inspired by an antique one, is perfect for a national celebration.

78

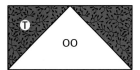

Templates: T, OO, PP, RR

Flying Geese Block
Finished size: 2" x 4"

MATERIALS

Yardage is based on 42"-wide fabric.

⭐ 1⅜ yds. white-on-white print for center block and fourth, fifth, sixth, and eleventh borders

⭐ Assorted pink, red, burgundy, blue, medium blue, blue-gray, brown, light gold, dark gold, cream, green, and olive green prints and solids for appliqués

⭐ 1 yd. blue print for bird appliqué, fifth and eleventh borders, and binding

⭐ ¼ yd. green print for first and third borders

⭐ ¼ yd. white-with-light-green print for second border

⭐ ½ yd. red solid for first and third border corner squares, and seventh and ninth borders

⭐ ⅝ yd. green paisley for eighth border

⭐ ⅜ yd. light gold solid for tenth border

⭐ 1½ yds. fabric for backing

⭐ 45" x 45" square of thin batting

⭐ Green embroidery floss

CUTTING

The following steps list rotary cutting measurements. When available, template letters for hand piecing are shown in parentheses; some pieces are quite large and would require template patterns in sizes too big to fit in the book.

1. From the white-on-white print, cut:
   - 1 square, 14½" x 14½", for the center block
   - 56 rectangles, 2½" x 4½", or 56 large triangles (template OO), for fifth and eleventh border flying-geese units
   - 4 squares, 2⅞" x 2⅞". Cut each square once diagonally to yield 8 triangles for fifth and eleventh border half-square-triangle units. Or, cut 8 triangles (template T).

2. From the blue print, cut:
   - 112 squares, 2½" x 2½", or 112 small triangles (template T), for fifth and eleventh border flying-geese units
   - 4 squares, 2⅞" x 2⅞". Cut each square once diagonally to yield 8 triangles for fifth and eleventh border half-square-triangle units. Or, cut 8 triangles (template T).

3. From the red solid, cut:
   - 4 squares (template RR), 1" x 1", for first border
   - 4 squares (template PP), 1½" x 1½", for third border

QUILT-TOP ASSEMBLY

1. Refer to "Appliquéing" on page 12 to cut the appliqué pieces on pages 82–85 from the fabrics indicated and appliqué them to the center block in the order indicated, using your favorite method. Refer to "Embroidering" on page 13 to stem stitch the leaf stems with green embroidery floss. Trim the block to 13½" x 13½".

2. For the first border, measure the center block as described in "Adding Borders" on page 14. Measure for the side *and* top and bottom borders. From the green print, cut 2 strips, each 1" wide by the length measured, and 2 strips, 1" wide by the width measured. Stitch the side borders to the sides of the quilt top. Press the seams toward the borders. Stitch a 1" red solid corner square (template RR) to the ends of the remaining 2 strips. Stitch the pieced border strips to the top and bottom edges of the quilt top. Press the seams toward the borders.

3. For the second border, measure the quilt top as described in "Adding Borders" on page 14. From the white-with-light-green print, cut 1½"-wide strips to the lengths measured and stitch them to the quilt top.

4. Repeat step 2 for the third border, cutting 1½"-wide strips from the green print fabric and adding the 1½" red squares (template PP) to the top and bottom borders.

5. For the fourth border, measure the quilt top and cut 1½"-wide strips from the white-on-white print to the lengths measured; stitch them to the quilt top.

6. If you rotary cut the pieces, refer to "Flying Geese" on page 18 to make 56 flying-geese units with the white 2½" x 4½" rectangles and the blue print 2½" x 2½" squares. If you used templates, sew small blue triangles (template T) to each short side of each large white triangle (template OO).

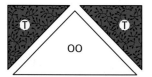 

Make 56.

7. Stitch each blue print triangle (template T) to a white-on-white print triangle (template T). Make 8 half-square-triangle units.

8. To make the pieced fifth border, stitch 5 flying-geese units together as shown. Make 4 strips.

Make 4.

9. Stitch 2 of the pieced border strips to the sides of the quilt top as shown. Stitch a half-square-triangle unit from step 7 to the ends of the remaining 2 pieced strips as shown. Stitch the strips to the top and bottom edges of the quilt top.

10. For each of the sixth through tenth borders, measure the quilt top for borders as described in "Adding Borders" on page 14. Cut the strips to the lengths measured and stitch them to the quilt top. For the sixth border, cut 1½"-wide strips from the white-on-white print. For the seventh border, cut 1"-wide strips from the red solid. For the eighth border, cut 4"-wide strips from the green paisley. For the ninth border, cut 1"-wide strips from the red solid. For the tenth border, cut 1"-wide strips from the light gold solid.

11. For the eleventh border, sew 9 flying-geese units together as shown. Make 4 strips.

Make 4.

12. Stitch 2 of the pieced border strips to the sides of the quilt top as shown. Stitch a half-square-triangle unit from step 7 to the ends of the remaining 2 pieced strips as shown. Stitch the strips to the top and bottom edges of the quilt top.

QUILT FINISHING
Refer to "Quilt Finishing" on pages 14–16.

1. Layer the quilt top with batting and backing; baste.
2. Quilt as desired.
3. Bind the edges of the quilt.
4. Tea dye if desired.
5. Press the quilt.

Quilting Suggestion

Outline-quilt around the appliqués and the flying-geese border pieces. Quilt in the ditch of each border and fill the paisley border with a diagonal grid.

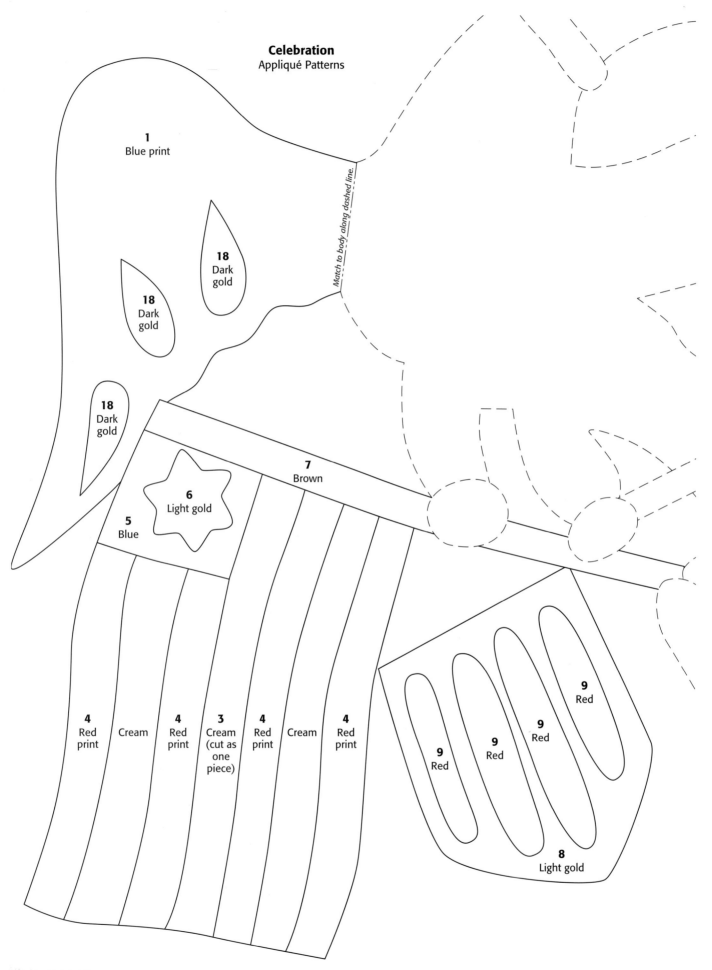

Celebration
Appliqué Patterns

1
Blue print

18
Dark gold

18
Dark gold

18
Dark gold

Match to body along dashed line.

7
Brown

6
Light gold

5
Blue

9
Red

9
Red

9
Red

9
Red

9
Red

8
Light gold

4
Red print

Cream

4
Red print

3
Cream (cut as one piece)

4
Red print

Cream

4
Red print

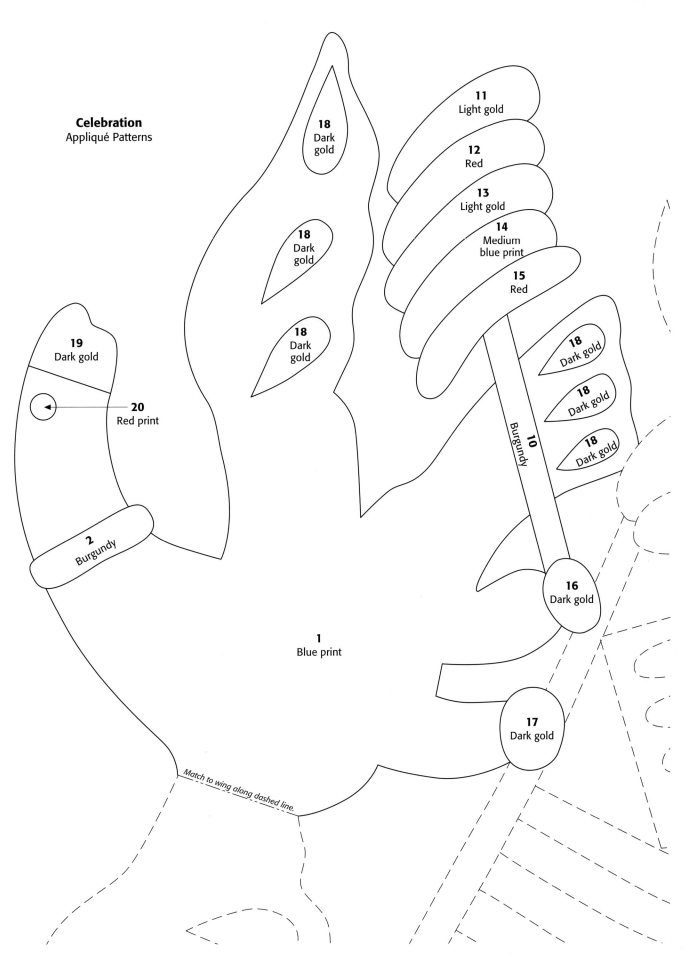

Celebration
Appliqué Patterns

11 Light gold

12 Red

13 Light gold

14 Medium blue print

15 Red

18 Dark gold

18 Dark gold

18 Dark gold

18 Dark gold

10 Burgundy

18 Dark gold

18 Dark gold

19 Dark gold

20 Red print

2 Burgundy

16 Dark gold

1 Blue print

17 Dark gold

Match to wing along dashed line.

Celebration
Appliqué Patterns

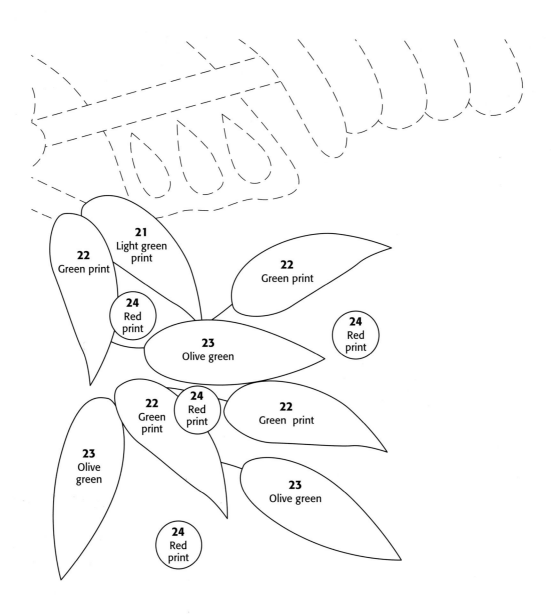

Celebration
Appliqué Patterns

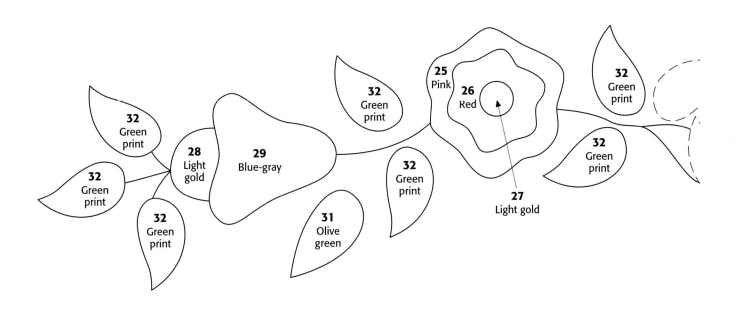

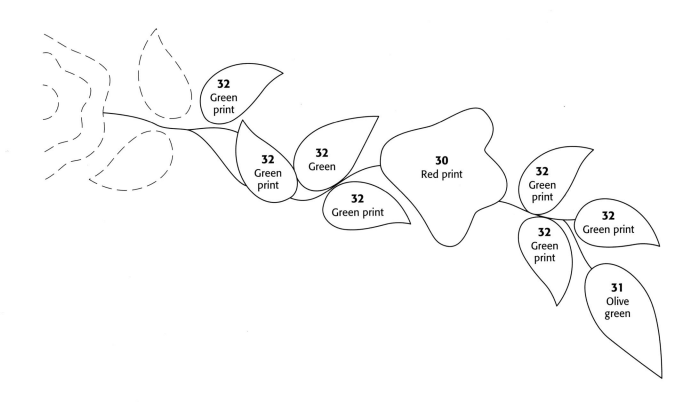

Little Quilt Flags

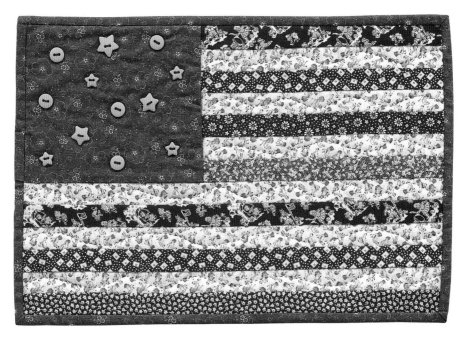

By Alice Berg, 2002, Marietta, Georgia, 10¼" x 15½".

By Tina Schuman, 2002, Marietta, Georgia, 10¼" x 15½".

Quilted flags are really fun to make, and these spirited Little Quilts are easy to adapt to your own personal taste! Use your favorite red, white, and blue colors; then let your imagination run wild when embellishing the flag star field. Our instructions that follow explain how to embellish the flag star field with the Stitchery Sue embroidery pattern, but you can also consider decorating it with things like buttons, machine embroidery, or quilting designs. Or create a design that represents a country that is part of your heritage and place it in the star field.

Consider alternative designs for your flag
star field, such as the examples shown here.

MATERIALS

Yardage is based on 42"-wide fabric.

⭐ 6" x 7" rectangle of fabric for flag star field

⭐ ¼ yd. *total* assorted fabrics for red stripes

⭐ ¼ yd. *total* assorted fabrics for white stripes

⭐ ⅝ yd. fabric for backing

⭐ ¼ yd. fabric for binding

⭐ 15" x 20" rectangle of thin batting

⭐ Red embroidery floss

CUTTING

1. From the assorted fabrics for red stripes, cut:
   - 4 strips, 1¼" x 9½"*, for upper stripes
   - 3 strips, 1¼" x 15½"*, for lower stripes
2. From the assorted fabrics for white stripes, cut:
   - 3 strips, 1¼" x 9½"*, for upper stripes
   - 3 strips, 1¼" x 15½"*, for lower stripes

*Refer to "Successful Stripes" on page 88 to cut strips
longer if desired.*

QUILT-TOP ASSEMBLY

1. Trace the Stitchery Sue embroidery pattern on page 88 to the right side of the flag star field rectangle, using a fine-tip water-soluble marker. Refer to "Embroidering" on page 13 to embroider the design with red floss. Work cross-stitch for the flag stars and double cross-stitch for the dress stars; stem stitch the remaining lines. Follow the manufacturer's instructions to remove the markings. Trim the stitched rectangle to 5¾" x 6½", keeping the design centered.

2. Alternately stitch the 1¼" x 9½" red and white strips together along the long edge, beginning and ending with a red strip, to make the flag upper stripes. Repeat with the 1¼" x 15½" red and white strips, beginning with a white strip and ending with a red strip, to make the flag lower stripes.

3. Stitch the flag upper stripes, lower stripes, and flag star field together as shown.

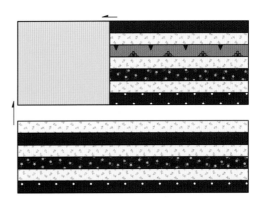

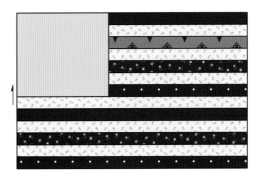

QUILT FINISHING

Refer to "Quilt Finishing" on pages 14–16.

1. Layer the quilt top with batting and backing; baste.
2. Quilt wavy lines on the stripes.
3. Bind the edges of the quilt.
4. Tea dye if desired.
5. Embellish with buttons, beads, or other materials if desired.

Stitchery Sue
Embroidery Pattern

Successful Stripes

No matter how we try, it's difficult to sew several "cut-to-size" strips together without having uneven edges. To have sections fit properly, cut the strips longer, sew them together, and then trim them to the size needed. Cut fabric on the lengthwise grain to avoid stretching and rippling.

Pressing as you sew is also important. Sew 2 strips together, press the seam flat, and then press the seam toward the darker fabric.

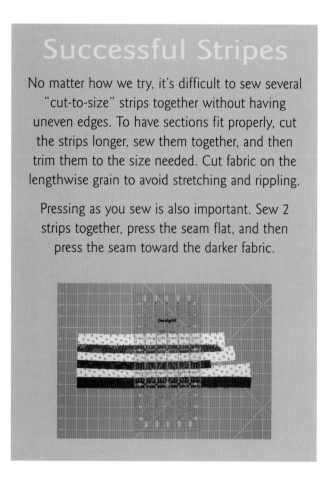

Template Patterns

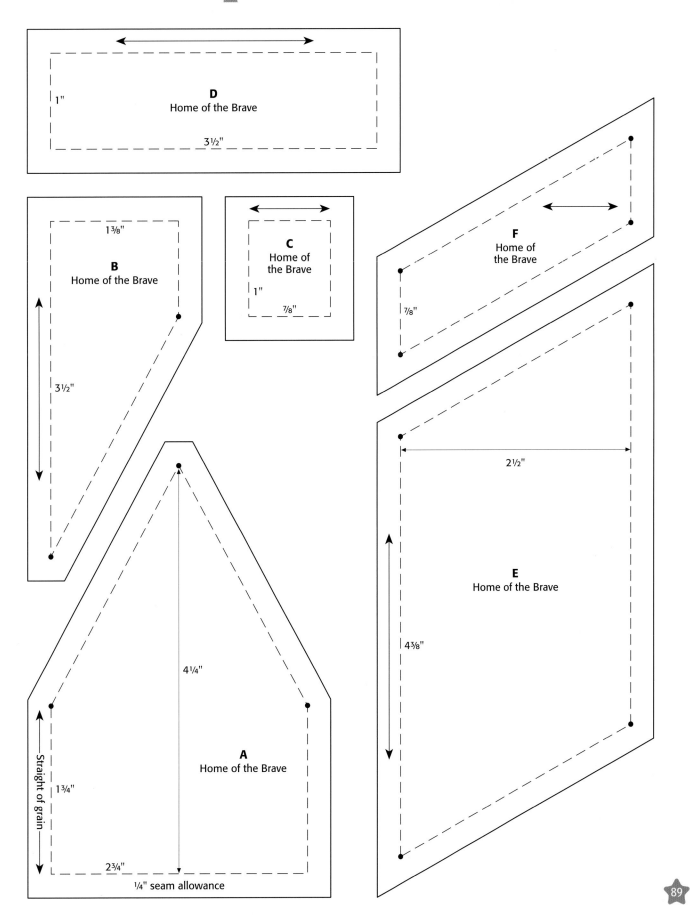

D
Home of the Brave

1"

3½"

B
Home of the Brave

1⅜"

3½"

C
Home of
the Brave

1"

⅞"

F
Home of
the Brave

⅞"

2½"

E
Home of the Brave

4⅜"

A
Home of the Brave

4¼"

Straight of grain

1¾"

2¾"

¼" seam allowance

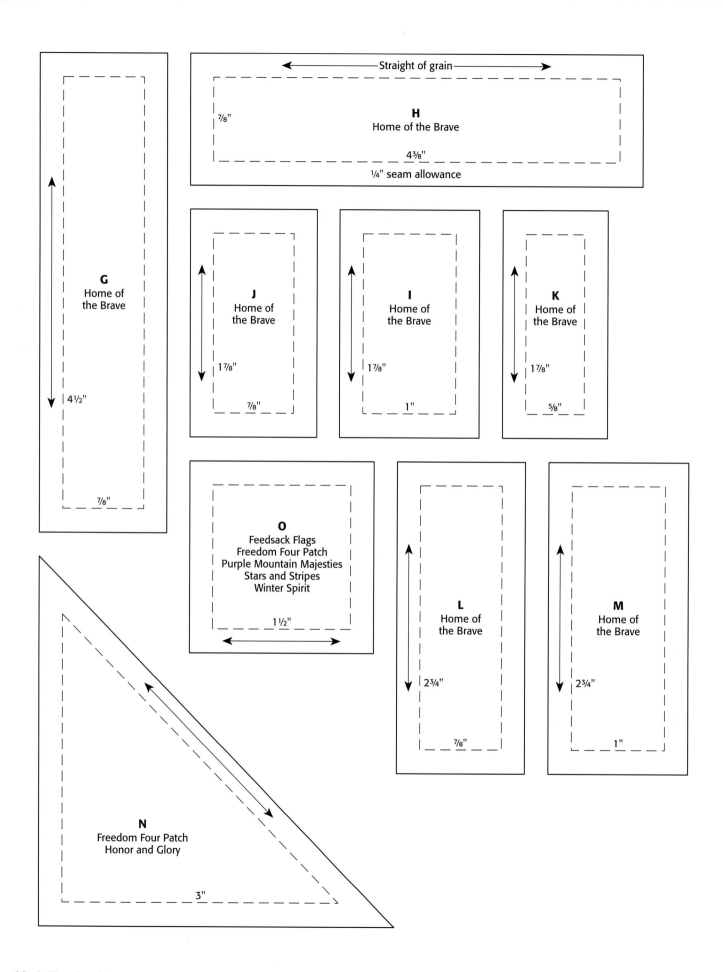

Straight of grain

H
Home of the Brave

7/8"

4 3/8"

1/4" seam allowance

G
Home of
the Brave

4 1/2"

7/8"

J
Home of
the Brave

1 7/8"

7/8"

I
Home of
the Brave

1 7/8"

1"

K
Home of
the Brave

1 7/8"

5/8"

O
Feedsack Flags
Freedom Four Patch
Purple Mountain Majesties
Stars and Stripes
Winter Spirit

1 1/2"

L
Home of
the Brave

2 3/4"

7/8"

M
Home of
the Brave

2 3/4"

1"

N
Freedom Four Patch
Honor and Glory

3"

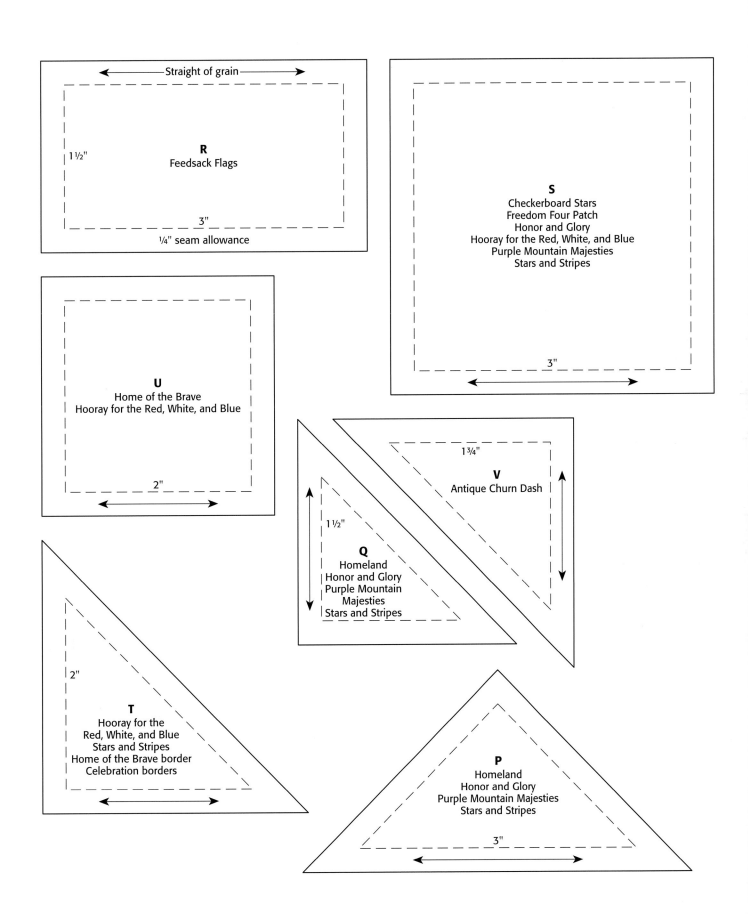

Straight of grain

R
Feedsack Flags

1 ½"

3"

¼" seam allowance

S
Checkerboard Stars
Freedom Four Patch
Honor and Glory
Hooray for the Red, White, and Blue
Purple Mountain Majesties
Stars and Stripes

3"

U
Home of the Brave
Hooray for the Red, White, and Blue

2"

1 ¾"

V
Antique Churn Dash

1 ½"

Q
Homeland
Honor and Glory
Purple Mountain
Majesties
Stars and Stripes

2"

T
Hooray for the
Red, White, and Blue
Stars and Stripes
Home of the Brave border
Celebration borders

P
Homeland
Honor and Glory
Purple Mountain Majesties
Stars and Stripes

3"

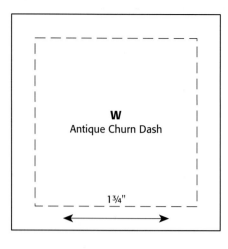

W
Antique Churn Dash

1¾"

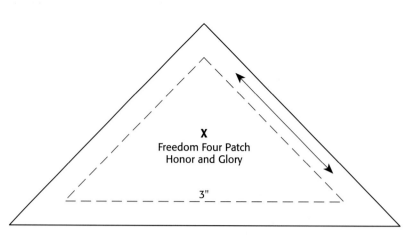

X
Freedom Four Patch
Honor and Glory

3"

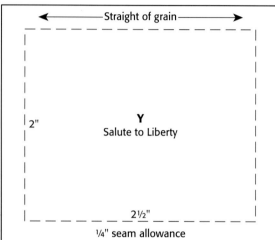

Straight of grain

2"

Y
Salute to Liberty

2½"

¼" seam allowance

½"

Z
Homeland
Salute to Liberty

3½"

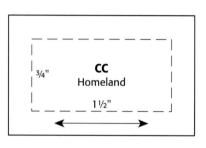

¾"

CC
Homeland

1½"

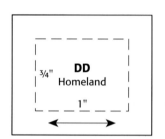

¾"

DD
Homeland

1"

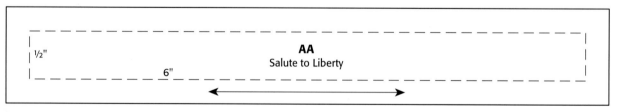

½"

AA
Salute to Liberty

6"

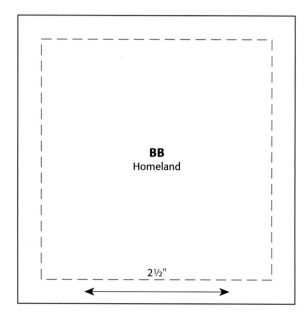

BB
Homeland

2½"

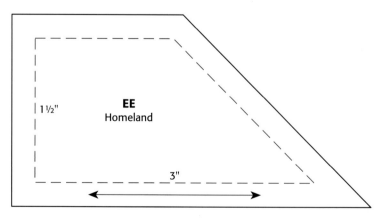

1½"

EE
Homeland

3"

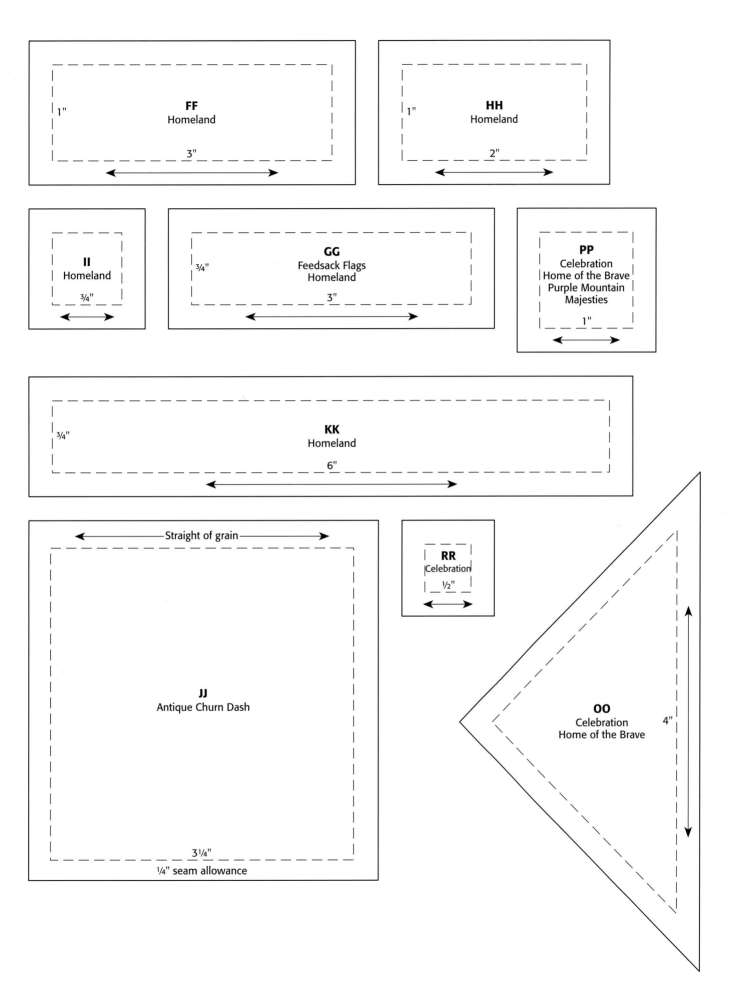

FF
Homeland
1"
3"

HH
Homeland
1"
2"

II
Homeland
3/4"
3/4"

GG
Feedsack Flags
Homeland
3/4"
3"

PP
Celebration
Home of the Brave
Purple Mountain
Majesties
1"

KK
Homeland
3/4"
6"

Straight of grain

JJ
Antique Churn Dash
3 1/4"
1/4" seam allowance

RR
Celebration
1/2"

OO
Celebration
Home of the Brave
4"

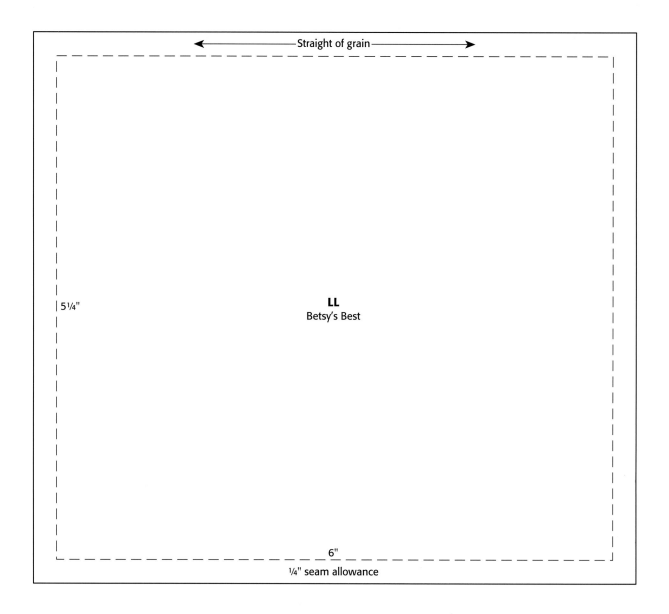

Straight of grain

5¼"

LL
Betsy's Best

6"
¼" seam allowance

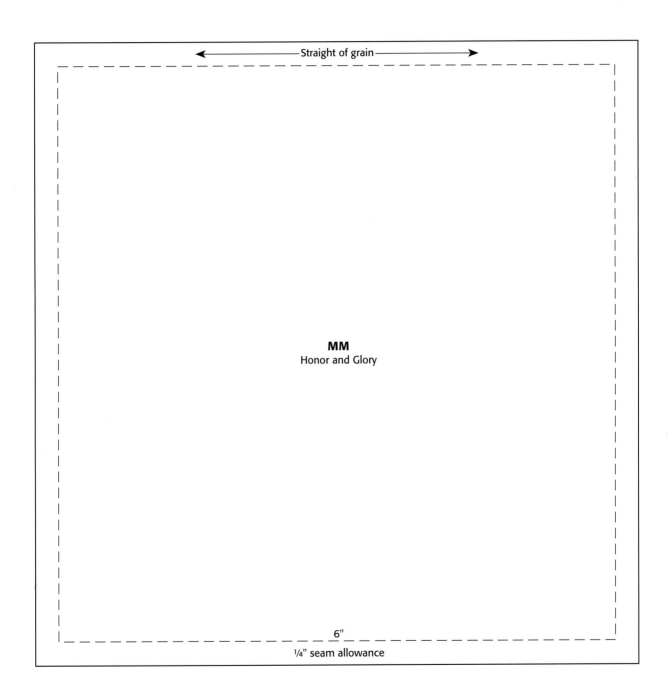

Straight of grain

MM
Honor and Glory

6"

¼" seam allowance

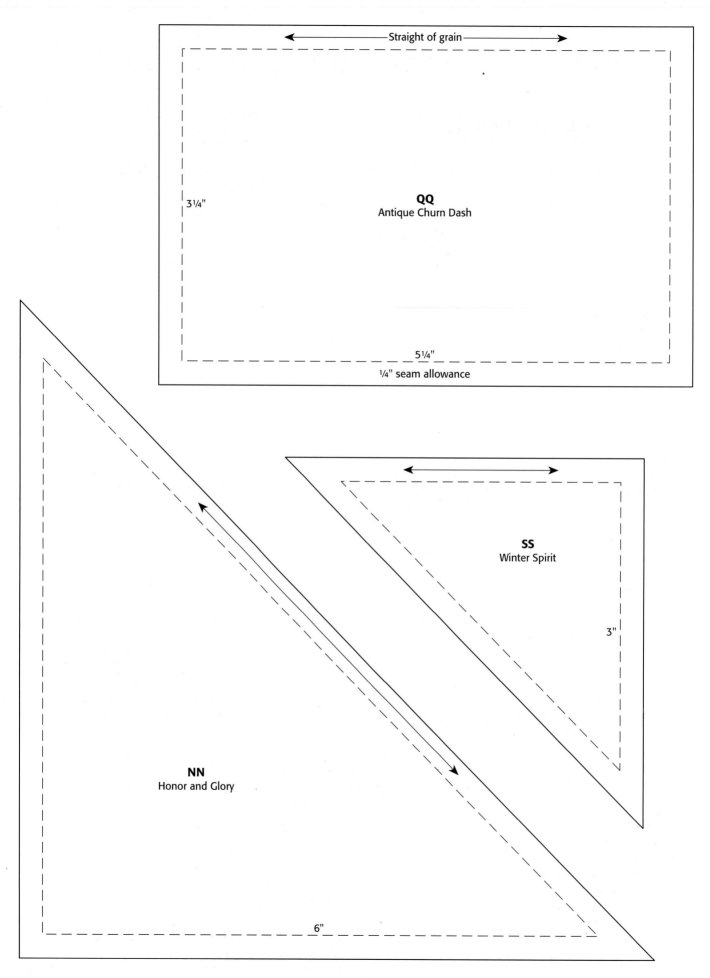

Straight of grain

QQ
Antique Churn Dash

3¼"

5¼"

¼" seam allowance

SS
Winter Spirit

3"

NN
Honor and Glory

6"